The RDA Workbook

Learning the Basics of Resource Description and Access

Margaret Mering, Editor

LIBRARIES UNLIMITED

AN IMPRINT OF ABC-CLIO, LLC
Santa Barbara, California • Denver, Colorado • Oxford, England

Copyright 2014 by Margaret Mering

Library of Congress Cataloging-in-Publication Data

The RDA workbook : learning the basics of resource description and access / Margaret Mering, editor.
  pages cm
Includes bibliographical references and index.
  ISBN 978-1-61069-489-6 (pbk.) – ISBN 978-1-61069-490-2 (ebook) 1. Resource description & access.
2. Descriptive cataloging–Standards. 3. Descriptive cataloging–Standards–Problems, exercises, etc.
I. Mering, Margaret, editor of compilation.
Z694.15.R47R33   2014
025.3'2—dc23   2013042469

ISBN: 978–1–61069–489–6
EISBN: 978–1–61069–490–2

18 17 16 15 14   2 3 4 5

This book is also available on the World Wide Web as an eBook.
Visit www.abc-clio.com for details.

Libraries Unlimited
An Imprint of ABC-CLIO, LLC

ABC-CLIO, LLC
130 Cremona Drive, P.O. Box 1911
Santa Barbara, California 93116-1911

This book is printed on acid-free paper ∞

Manufactured in the United States of America

WorldCat Records used in this book were extracted from OCLC's WorldCat database. Copyright © OCLC Online Computer Library Center, Inc. Used with OCLC's permission. OCLC and WorldCat are registered trademarks/service marks of OCLC.

Selected definitions and phrases from the FRBR and ICP (Statement of International Cataloging Principles) documents are used with permission from The International Federation of Library Associations and Institutions (IFLA).

RDA: Resource Description and Access © 2010—American Library Association, Canadian Library Association, and CILIP: Chartered Institute of Library and Information Professionals. Used by permission of the Co-Publishers of RDA (American Library Association, Canadian Library Association, and CILIP: Chartered Institute of Library and Information Professionals).

The RDA Workbook

Contents

2   RDA in the Real World: Preparing Bibliographic Records 39

*Corinne Jacox, Margaret Mering, Melissa Moll, Emily Dust Nimsakont, and
Deirdre Routt*

List of Figures

CD Contents

Exercises

Answers to Exercises

Sample MARC Records Following RDA Instructions

Quick Guides

Worksheet 4.1   Factoring Staff Time and Cost

Introduction

On March 31, 2013, the Library of Congress officially began using *RDA: Resource Description and Access* for all its original cataloging, replacing the *Anglo-American Cataloguing Rules (2nd ed.)*. Also, since this date, all records added to the Library of Congress / Name Authority Cooperative Program authority file must be created according to RDA instructions. As of the writing of this workbook, two months have passed since this historic day. While the Library of Congress, the National Agricultural Library, the National Library of Medicine, national libraries of other countries, and several large academic libraries have made the transition to the new standard for cataloging, many libraries of all types and sizes are in the middle of implementing RDA or are considering what steps to take toward this goal.

This workbook is intended for a general audience that may come from public, college, special, or school libraries. It provides a basic introduction to RDA and suggestions for implementing RDA. It is not meant to be comprehensive. The print version of this workbook includes a book and an accompanying CD-ROM.

The book includes four chapters. The first chapter reviews the theoretical framework of RDA, including the Functional Requirements for Bibliographic Records (FRBR) and the Statement of International Cataloguing Principles. The second chapter outlines essential highlights of RDA and provides a comparison with AACR2. It builds a bibliographic record for *The Literacy Cookbook*, a simple printed book. The third chapter introduces elements of authorized access points of persons, families, corporate bodies, works, and expressions. It explains how to read and interpret authority records. The final chapter suggests ways of implementing RDA locally in three phases.

The workbook also includes exercises, quick guides, and a glossary of terms. Mini-exercises are found throughout the chapter. Longer exercises corresponding to each chapter are found at the end of each chapter and on the accompanying CD-ROM. The quick guides provide ready-reference information as you learn about RDA. For ease of use, the longer exercises and the quick guides can be printed out from the accompanying CD-ROM.

This publication is the product of the hard work and dedication of many individuals. The inspiration for this book began with Casey Kralik and Corinne Jacox exchanging email messages about RDA-related topics found on listserv discussions. Their email exchanges led Kralik to form the Nebraska RDA Practice Group. This group met monthly from February 2012 to May 2013. It attracted members from university, college, public, school, and special libraries from the Lincoln and Omaha areas and as far west as Hastings, Nebraska. It also provided opportunities for librarians to become familiar with RDA and to help plan the implementation of RDA at their own local institutions. Special thanks are given to Sue Ann Gardner and Robin Bernstein for writing an article about the group's work for *Library Journal,* which led to ABC-CLIO contacting us about creating this workbook (Gardner and Bernstein 2012). Thanks are also given to Andrea Cotton, Angela Kroeger, Denise Matulka, Vicki Perrie, Jill Sempek, Mary Tilley, and other members of the Nebraska RDA Practice Group who tested exercises, found examples, and reviewed each chapter of the workbook.

We dedicate this workbook to the catalogers from the Nebraska RDA Practice Group and to you, our readers. We hope this publication furthers your understanding of RDA and assists you with your own local implementation of RDA.

Acronyms

AACR2	Anglo-American Cataloguing Rules, second edition
ALCTS	Association for Library Collections and Technical Services
BIBFRAME	Bibliographic Framework
FRAD	Functional Requirements for Authority Data
FRBR	Functional Requirements for Bibliographic Records
FRSAR	Functional Requirements for Subject Authority Records
GMD	General Material Designation
ICP	Statement of International Cataloguing Principles
IFLA	International Federation of Library Associations and Institutions
ILS	Integrated Library System
ISBD	International Standard Bibliographic Description
JSC	Joint Steering Committee for Development of RDA
LC	Library of Congress
LC-PCC	Library of Congress-Program for Cooperative Cataloging
LC-PCC PS	Library of Congress-Program for Cooperative Cataloging Policy Statements
MARC	MAchine-Readable Cataloging
NACO	Name Authority Cooperative Program
OLAC	Online Audiovisual Catalogers
OPAC	Online Public Access Catalog
OCLC	Online Computer Library Center
PCC	Program for Cooperative Cataloging
RDA	Resource Description and Access
WEMI	Work, Expression, Manifestation, and Item

1

FRBR, the Framework behind RDA

Melissa Moll

We live in an era of connections. Our digital devices connect us to communications networks. Websites and social media tools connect shoppers with retailers, information seekers with information providers, and like-minded individuals with each other. As methods of linking online data evolve, connections and relationships between people, places, organizations, resources, and ideas become pathways to navigate webs of information.

Cataloging has always highlighted connections, linking authors, titles, subjects, and publication details within the context of a bibliographic record. *Resource Description and Access* (RDA) and *Functional Requirements for Bibliographic Records* (FRBR) continue this focus on connections and relationships, asking questions such as:

How do resources relate to each other?
How do creators and subjects relate to those resources?
How can we help users connect to and acquire the resources they need and want?

These are not new questions, but RDA and FRBR attempt to answer them in a way that offers new possibilities for library catalogs and library users in our connected, digital world.

Goals for Chapter 1:
- Reflect on the user focus of FRBR and the Statement of International Cataloging Principles.
- Understand the basic conceptual framework of FRBR, including entities, attributes, and relationships.
- Navigate within the FRBR-ized structure of RDA.

User Focus, User Convenience, and User Tasks

Who are the users of a catalog? They include patrons of all ages and from all walks of life who enter physical or digital library doors; seekers of information housed in archives, museums, and organizations with similar missions; and librarians, copy catalogers, and other professionals who create, share, and utilize bibliographic and authority records. All of these users share a common overarching need: catalogs that effectively, efficiently, and successfully execute their information-seeking tasks.

What are the needs of these catalog users? Released by the International Federation of Library Associations and Institutions (IFLA) in 2009, the *Statement of International Cataloguing Principles* (ICP) places primary importance on "the convenience of the user" (ICP 2.1; see Figure 1.1). It reflects and builds on

Figure 1.1
General Principles from the Statement of International Cataloguing Principles (ICP)

---

1. Convenience of the user.
Decisions taken in the making of descriptions and controlled forms of names for access should be made with the user in mind.

2. Common usage.
Vocabulary used in descriptions and access should be in accord with that of the majority of users.

3. Representation.
Descriptions and controlled forms of names should be based on the way an entity describes itself.

4. Accuracy.
The entity described should be faithfully portrayed.

5. Sufficiency and necessity.
Only those data elements in descriptions and controlled forms of names for access that are required to fulfill user tasks and are essential to uniquely identify an entity should be included.

6. Significance.
Data elements should be bibliographically significant.

7. Economy.
When alternative ways exist to achieve a goal, preference should be given to the way that best furthers overall economy (i.e., the least cost or the simplest approach).

8. Consistency and standardization.
Descriptions and construction of access points should be standardized as far as possible. This enables greater consistency, which in turn increases the ability to share bibliographic and authority data.

9. Integration.
The descriptions for all types of materials and controlled forms of names of all types of entities should be based on a common set of rules, insofar as it is relevant.

Source: ICP 2.1-2.9

previous documents, including FRBR and the statement of principles developed by the International Conference on Cataloguing Principles in 1961 (known as the *Paris Principles*). The ICP re-envisions the Paris Principles for a twenty-first-century online environment and an ever-increasing multitude of formats and types of materials (ICP p. 1). These

accounts for different [handwritten margin note]

Mini-Exercise 1.1

A patron enters your library ...

A patron enters your library. She needs a copy of *Old Jules* by Mari Sandoz for a school report. Follow her search from start to finish. What steps will she take so that she can leave the library with a copy of the book (either print or electronic)? How might her steps correspond to the user tasks of *find–identify–select–obtain–navigate–understand*?

Note: This mini-exercise does not have a single definitive answer. Consider your own library setting and trace the path that a typical patron takes to complete the user tasks.

principles serve as a mission and vision statement, a foundational document guiding the international cataloging community forward.

FRBR outlines four general user tasks: *find, identify, select,* and *obtain* (FRBR 6.1). For example, users want to find Audrey Wood's *The Napping House* or all of the books a library has by Jonathan Franzen. Offered multiple editions of a book, users identify which edition they want. Scrolling through the library website late one night, they select the eBook format so that they can finish a report due the following day. Wandering through the stacks, they acquire or obtain a DVD copy of their favorite movie.

The ICP adds the need for users to easily *navigate* within and through a catalog (ICP 4.5). Are the arrangement, presentation, and overall information architecture of the catalog clear? Does the catalog point users to related resources or people? RDA also notes the need of users to *understand* (RDA 0.4.2.1). From the catalog records, can a user quickly comprehend that Resource A is the sequel to Resource B, or that Corporation X used to have a different name?

Find–Identify–Select–Obtain–Navigate–Understand. These foundational user tasks become a cornerstone for cataloging.

Svenonius [handwritten margin note]

The Three Cs: Concept, Content, and Container

The Concept of FRBR

FRBR is a *concept*—a conceptual framework or model that organizes and arranges the resources, beings, and subjects of the bibliographic universe. The genesis of FRBR came at the 1990 Stockholm Seminar on Bibliographic Records, and IFLA formally accepted the FRBR report in 1997 (FRBR 1.1-2). Two subsequent documents, *Functional Requirements for Authority Data* (FRAD) and *Functional Requirements for Subject Authority Data* (FRSAD), expand the FRBR model.

Figure 1.2
Entity-Relationship Model Basics

FRBR (often pronounced *fer-ber*) borrows the techniques and vocabulary of the entity-relationship model used in database design. The entity-relationship model organizes data using three basic constructs: *entities, attributes,* and *relationships* (see Figure 1.2). The entities are the things, the objects, the people, the places, the concepts, and so on. Entities can be concrete or abstract, animate or inanimate. Entities have attributes—characteristics that describe the entities and distinguish one entity from another. Entities also exist in relationship to each other. These relationships tie the entities together in specific, defined ways (Chen 1976, 10–12). Borrowing from the language of grammar, entities represent the nouns; attributes, the descriptive adjectives; and relationships, the verbs that bind everything together.

Imagine that you are constructing a database of the solar system. The entities in your database would include *Sun* and *Earth*. Attributes of the *Earth* entity could include type of body (terrestrial planet), circumference (around 40,075 km at the equator), and number of moons (one). The two entities *Sun* and *Earth* also relate to each other: the *Earth* orbits the *Sun,* and the *Sun* is orbited by the *Earth.*

FRBR is one method of explaining the bibliographic universe—that confluence of ideas, objects, resources, people, places, subjects, and more. Following the entity-relationship model, FRBR defines the entities (the ideas, objects, etc.) that comprise the bibliographic universe, identifies the attributes or characteristics associated with each entity, and describes the relationships between the entities (FRBR 1.2). As is the nature of a model, the real-world application of FRBR may work better in some situations than in others.

Consider the galaxy within the bibliographic universe surrounding *The Adventures of Tom Sawyer.* We know that Samuel Langhorne Clemens, writing as Mark Twain, conceived the idea of a story about the antics of a boy named

Tom growing up in the fictional Mississippi River town of St. Petersburg, Missouri. The story was originally published in 1876 as a book in the English language. In the intervening years, numerous editors, illustrators, and publishers have issued Tom's story in regular print editions, large print editions, braille books, microforms, eBooks, and audiobooks. The audiobooks alone are available as LPs, cassettes, CDs, and downloadable audiobooks. Translators have retold the story in German, Spanish, French, Chinese, Dutch, Korean, Afrikaans, and many other languages. *The Adventures of Tom Sawyer* has also inspired related dissertations, articles, kits, musical scores, motion pictures, and interactive multimedia resources. Mark Twain's story has even been adapted for the zombie world as seen in *The Adventures of Tom Sawyer and the Undead* by Don Borchert. The *Tom Sawyer* galaxy is indeed rich, complex, and ever-expanding.

FRBR links the stars, planets, moons, comets, and black holes of the *Tom Sawyer* galaxy to organize this section of the bibliographic universe. The ideas, resources, people, places, and concepts connected to *Tom Sawyer* become a web leading users from one entity to another. FRBR divides all of these swirling entities into three groups (FRBR 3.1; FRAD Figure 2):

- Group 1 Entities: Work, Expression, Manifestation, and Item
- Group 2 Entities: Person, Family, and Corporate Body
- Group 3 Entities: Concept, Object, Event, and Place

Within the *Tom Sawyer* galaxy, the Group 1 entities include Mark Twain's idea of a story about a young boy (a work); that story realized through the original written English text or through spoken words (expressions); a 135th anniversary edition of the English text published by the University of California Press in 2010 (a manifestation); and a copy of the 135th anniversary edition at the Northeast Community College Library in Norfolk, Nebraska (an item). Group 2 entities linked to the *Tom Sawyer* galaxy include Samuel Clemens, the pseudonymous Mark Twain, and Don Borchert (persons), while runaway children (a concept) and the Mississippi River valley (a place) represent Group 3 entities.

FRBR also explicitly states the relationships between entities. Thus, the work *The Adventures of Tom Sawyer* has an author Mark Twain; reciprocally, Mark Twain is the author of *The Adventures of Tom Sawyer*. The work *The Adventures of Tom Sawyer* has as expressions the author's original English text as well as an Italian translation by Bruno Oddera titled *Le avventure di Tom Sawyer*. Also, the work *The Adventures of Tom Sawyer* is the basis for the related work *The Adventures of Tom Sawyer and the Undead*.

In FRBR, entities are described and differentiated through their attributes. Dates of a person (such as date of birth or date of death) are one attribute of the Group 2 entity *person* (FRBR 4.6.2). For example, the Samuel Clemens who wrote as Mark Twain was born in 1835 and died in 1910. These dates help to distinguish him from his grandfather, also named Samuel Clemens, who was born around 1770 and died in 1805. Within FRBR, attributes, relationships, and entities chart the bibliographic universe, with the aim of linking users to galaxies of information.

The Content of RDA

While FRBR remains a concept, RDA focuses on *content*. RDA is the standard that provides the guidelines or instructions to apply when cataloging. It builds on and fleshes out the FRBR model. As stated in the introductory chapter of RDA, FRBR and FRAD stand at the core of RDA as its theoretical foundation:

> A key element in the design of RDA is its alignment with the conceptual models for bibliographic and authority data developed by the International Federation of Library Associations and Institutions (IFLA). The FRBR and FRAD models provide RDA with an underlying framework that has the scope needed to support comprehensive coverage of all types of content and media, the flexibility and extensibility needed to accommodate newly emerging resource characteristics, and the adaptability needed for the data produced to function within a wide range of technological environments. (RDA 0.3.1)

The adjectives *comprehensive, flexible, extensible,* and *adaptable* from the preceding paragraph outline some of the fundamental characteristics and goals of RDA. Library collections continue to expand the range of formats available to patrons, offering print to digital to three-dimensional objects and everything in between. A twenty-first-century cataloging standard thus needs a comprehensive scope able to expand and encompass future formats that will emerge in five, fifteen, or fifty years. RDA breaks down bibliographic elements into multiple component parts but does not dictate how the information is displayed, permitting these small segments of data to adapt to a variety of online presentations. The qualities of flexibility and adaptability allow the content of RDA to evolve and remain applicable within new "technological environments" (RDA 0.3.1).

The Container of MARC

While FRBR is a concept and RDA focuses on content, formats such as MARC (MAchine-Readable Cataloging) provide a *container* for the bibliographic data. The fields and subfields of MARC communicate and package the content outlined by RDA. This container-neutral RDA content could likewise be transmitted through Dublin Core (DC), the Metadata Object Description Schema (MODS), or another metadata encoding scheme yet to come. The container may change, but the RDA content remains the same regardless of communication format.

Ideally, the concept of FRBR, the content of RDA, and containers for metadata encoding work together to shape bibliographic data into a form useful to library patrons, able to collocate related items, and designed to interact in a web-based environment. We then have the tools to more fully explore and exploit the bibliographic universe.

FRBR at the Grocery Store

As a way to examine the hierarchy of FRBR Group 1 entities within a nonlibrary context, imagine that you are walking into a grocery store at the start of a shopping trip. You pull a scribbled list out of your pocket: *milk, butter, eggs, bread.*

While strolling through the grocery store on the way to the bread aisle, you ponder what kind of bread to purchase that day. Perhaps a nice loaf of wheat bread or country white? Or would a loaf of French or Italian bread be better? Or should you buy a mix or a frozen loaf to bake at home? Then you remember a friend's recommendation of multigrain molasses bread, and your decision is made.

Within a few minutes, you are standing in the bread aisle before an array of choices, trying to decide between the oblong multigrain molasses loaves from the Best Bread Bakery and the round loaves from the Ultimate Bread Bakery. The oblong loaves seem fresher, so you choose one and add it to your cart.

Applying FRBR to grocery shopping may be a stretch, but the general principles apply. The word *bread* scribbled on your shopping list translates to the FRBR *work* entity—you know that you need to purchase something from the bread aisle. You have many types or *expressions* of bread from which to choose, including wheat, country white, French, and Italian. You decide on the expression of multigrain molasses bread but then encounter two *manifestations* sitting on the grocery store shelf—rows of oblong loaves from the Best Bread Bakery or round loaves from the Ultimate Bread Bakery. You select one of the oblong loaves—an *item* in FRBR terminology—and mark the word *bread* off your shopping list.

Notice that only when you reach the manifestation level do you have actual loaves of bread to place in your shopping cart. The work (bread) and expression (multigrain molasses) entities exist only as abstract ideas or concepts on your shopping list or in your mind. The tangible manifestation and item entities embody the intangible work and expression, becoming loaves of bread that you can see, touch, taste, and smell.

FRBR Group 1 Entities: Work, Expression, Manifestation, Item (WEMI)

According to FRBR, the Group 1 entities are "the products of intellectual or artistic endeavor that are named or described in bibliographic records" (FRBR 3.1). Works, expressions, manifestations, and items (referred to collectively by the acronym WEMI) are thus the creations and resources that we represent in catalog records and eventually make available for library patrons. FRBR defines the Group 1 entities as follows:

- *Work* (w): "a distinct intellectual or artistic creation" (FRBR 3.2.1)
- *Expression* (e): "the intellectual or artistic realization of a work in the form of alpha-numeric [written in letters and numbers], musical, or choreographic notation, sound, image, object, movement, etc., or any combination of such forms" (FRBR 3.2.2)
- *Manifestation* (m): "the physical embodiment of an expression of a work" (FRBR 3.2.3)
- *Item* (i): "a single exemplar of a manifestation" (FRBR 3.2.4)

Although patrons likely do not use the terms *work, expression, manifestation,* or *item,* they ask for resources at all four levels of the Group 1 entities. Patrons routinely come with questions and statements like the following:

- *Patron One:* "I'm looking for *Delights & Shadows* by the poet Ted Kooser."
- *Patron Two:* "Do you have a Spanish translation of Willa Cather's *O Pioneers!*?"
- *Patron Three:* "I would like to listen to *The Tao of Warren Buffett.* Can I access a downloadable audiobook?"
- *Patron Four:* "My toddler spilled grape juice all over the copy of *C is for Cornhusker: A Nebraska Alphabet* that we had checked out. Where do I pay the fine?"

Patron Four is discussing a specific copy or *item* that was checked out and now has grape juice stains. Patron Three's question comes directly at the *manifestation* level: a downloadable audiobook (the manifestation) with the spoken words (the expression) of *The Tao of Warren Buffet* (the work). Patron Two requests an *expression*: *O Pioneers!* (the work) as realized in a Spanish translation (the expression). Finally, Patron One is asking for a *work*—the creative poetic output by Ted Kooser known by the title *Delights & Shadows.* Notice that neither Patron One nor Patron Two requests a specific edition, format, or copy of a resource. Their two questions remain general, staying at the more nebulous level of the intellectual or creative content of a resource. In the course of fulfilling their requests, however, the reference librarian would lead the patrons down through the manifestation and finally the item levels. The patrons want to leave the library with a copy of the desired resource in hand.

In reality, no one sitting at a reference desk consciously (or even subconsciously) considers whether a patron request comes at the level of work, expression, manifestation, or item. In our daily lives, these four FRBR Group 1 entities tend to blend and blur. As a method of organizing the bibliographic universe,

Figure 1.3
FRBR Group 1 Entities and Primary Relationships

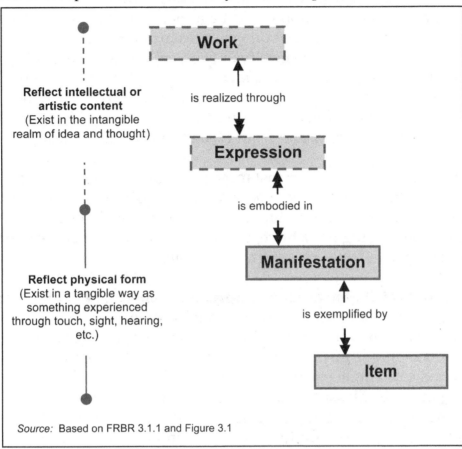

Source: Based on FRBR 3.1.1 and Figure 3.1

however, separating out the tiers highlights the connections binding together works, expressions, manifestations, and items.

Figure 1.3 shows the primary relationships between the Group 1 entities. In FRBR terms, a work *is realized through* an expression. An expression *is embodied in* (in other words, *made manifest in*) a manifestation. Using the vocabulary of RDA, this is the point at which the intellectual or creative *content* of the resource becomes housed within a physical *carrier* such as a computer disc or a monograph volume. Finally, a manifestation *is exemplified by* an individual item (FRBR 5.2.1).

The exact method of diagramming FRBR entities, attributes, and relationships may differ slightly between sources you consult. In this workbook, rectangles for work and expression entities have dotted lines, while those for manifestations and items have solid lines. This method distinguishes the intangible content of works and expressions from the physical forms of manifestations and items.

As shown in Figure 1.3, lines with either a single or a double arrow display the relationships between the entities. A single arrow equates to "one and only one," while a double arrow signifies "one or more than one" (FRBR 3.1.1). For example, a work may be realized through just one expression or through multiple expressions. A manifestation could be a mass-produced print run from a particular publisher, meaning that one manifestation can result in many, many items. An item, however, can exemplify only one manifestation. A library's copy of the 135th anniversary edition of *The Adventures of Tom Sawyer* published by the University of California Press in 2010 cannot simultaneously be a copy of the edition published by Houghton Mifflin in 1971. The publications from the University of California Press and from Houghton Mifflin represent two different manifestations.

An item is a specific copy or instance of a manifestation—*the* book, photograph, DVD, manuscript, eBook, and so on that you have in hand. Two items of the same manifestation, however, may not be completely identical. One copy of a book may be missing page three, while another might include handwritten annotations. One item could be designated for library use only, while the others can be checked out.

Much of our cataloging occurs at the manifestation level. Often, we catalog using a single item as an exemplar of its manifestation. The item we hold might come from a print run of thousands destined for the best-seller lists, or our item could be a single unique instance available only in our local collection. The manifestations tied to a single expression transmit the same intellectual or artistic content. Changes in physical format—from regular to large-print, or from DVD to Blu-ray—result in new manifestations. A recording of a favorite musical performance migrates from LP to cassette to compact disc to streaming audio, resulting in four manifestations of one expression. The publisher, or the year of publication, or the title on a title page changes, each time effecting a new manifestation.

FRBR describes an expression as "the specific intellectual or artistic form that a work takes each time it is 'realized'" (FRBR 3.2.2). A recording of your favorite musical work by Orchestra A will be a separate expression from a recording of that same musical work by Orchestra B. Although the two orchestras play the same notes, their interpretations (or *realizations*) of the musical work differ. In the same way, a Chinese translation of a novel by Translator A is a separate expression from a Chinese translation by Translator B. The original text of a work is a different expression than the revised text, an illustrated edition, or an abridged version. In all of these cases, a new performing group, a new translator, a revision of the text, added illustrations, or an abridgement changed the intellectual or artistic form and thus resulted in a new expression.

The boundaries between the Group 1 entities, especially between works and expressions, can sometimes be difficult to determine and definitively establish. For example, Person A could model two resources as separate works, while Person B could chart the same two resources in a work/expression relationship.

Different cultures, countries, or bibliographic communities may place the dividing line between works and expressions at varying points on the continuum of a family of works.

How much of the content is modified or changed from Resource A to Resource B? How much new intellectual or artistic effort is involved? These questions help to sort out works from expressions. An artist illustrates a classic children's story while leaving the text intact, resulting in a new expression of the same work. A writer adapts a novel into a screenplay, or a scholar produces an annotated edition of the Shakespeare sonnets, each time contributing significant artistic or intellectual effort and thus creating a new but related work. Perhaps a later reprint of a book does not change any of the original content, reflecting two manifestations of the same expression of a work. The degree of difference between Resource A and Resource B becomes an important factor when mapping works and expressions (Tillet 2004, 4).

Mini-Exercise 1.2

w, e, m, or i?

Categorize the following resources as works (w), expressions (e), manifestations (m), or items (i).

1. __i__   A copy of the CD recording of *The Adventures of Huckleberry Finn* (Saddleback Educational Publishing, 2011) in the library's Audiovisual Collection.

2. __e__   *The Adventures of Huckleberry Finn* in the original English text.

3. __m__   The book *The Adventures of Huckleberry Finn* published by Canterbury Classics in 2012.

4. __e__   *The Adventures of Huckleberry Finn* as spoken word in English.

5. __w__   The idea of Mark Twain's *The Adventures of Huckleberry Finn*.

6. __m__   The CD recording of *The Adventures of Huckleberry Finn* published in 2011 by Saddleback Educational Publishing.

7. __i__   A copy of the book *The Adventures of Huckleberry Finn* (Canterbury Classics, 2012) in the library's Young Adult Collection.

Attributes of Works, Expressions, Manifestations, and Items

Attributes help users find, identify, select, and obtain the resources they need and want. The attributes included in a bibliographic record gather and transmit the distinguishing characteristics of works, expressions, manifestations, and items. Figure 1.4 and Quick Guide 1.1 list selected attributes of the Group 1 entities. Some of these attributes apply only to certain subcategories such as cartographic materials, serials, microforms, sound recordings, musical scores, images, or hand-printed books. Other attributes are generally shared by most instances of that entity. For example, the attribute *form of expression* applies to all expressions, although the forms vary from alpha-numeric notation to musical sound to sculpture.

Figure 1.4
Selected Attributes of Group 1 Entities (WEMI)

Group 1 Entity	Selected Attributes
Work (w)	Title of the *work* Form of *work* (examples: novel, play, map) Date of the *work* Context for the *work* Other distinguishing characteristic of the *work* Intended audience Intended termination For musical works: medium of performance, numeric designation, key For cartographic works: coordinates, equinox
Expression (e)	Title of the *expression* Form of *expression* (examples: alpha-numeric notation, musical notation, spoken word, photographic image) Language of *expression* Extent of the *expression* (examples: duration, number of words) Summarization of content
Manifestation (m)	Title of the *manifestation* Statement of responsibility Edition/issue designation Place of publication/distribution Publisher/distributor Date of publication/distribution Fabricator/manufacturer Series statement Form of carrier Extent of the carrier Dimensions of the carrier *Manifestation* identifier (examples: ISBN, ISSN)
Item (i)	*Item* identifier (examples: a bar code, RFID tag, call number) Provenance of the *item* Marks/inscriptions Exhibition history Condition of the *item* Access restrictions on the *item*
See Quick Guide 1.1 for a more extensive list of FRBR/FRAD attributes and related RDA elements of Group 1 entities.	

FRBR attributes divide into two main types: intrinsic attributes that originate from within the entity and extrinsic attributes that originate outside the entity (FRBR 4.1). Consider all of the attributes gathered directly from a book sitting on a library shelf: title, statement of responsibility, publisher's name and place, number of pages, dimensions, the presence or absence of illustrations. All are intrinsic attributes or data elements garnered from the resource itself. Conversely, extrinsic attributes include the provenance of an item and access restrictions on a manifestation. Both of these examples depend on information external to the entity itself.

While FRBR borrows the word *attribute* from the entity-relationship model, RDA uses the term *element*. RDA defines an element as "a word, character, or group of words and/or characters representing a distinct unit of bibliographic information" (RDA Glossary). The RDA elements correlate to the FRBR attributes. For instance, the RDA element *content type* corresponds to the FRBR attribute *form of expression*.

As shown in Figure 1.5, attributes and relationships outlined in the FRBR model weave together to form bibliographic records. Chapter 2 of this workbook covers bibliographic records in more detail. Cataloging in a FRBR environment has the potential to increase efficiency. Attributes for a work may not need to be re-entered by a cataloger for each expression, or expression attributes for each manifestation, and so forth down to items. Thinking conversely from the bottom up, the bibliographic record for an item inherits the attributes of its manifestation; the manifestation inherits those of its expression; and the expression, those of its work (Tillet 2004, 6).

Works, Expressions, Manifestations, and Items in Practice

The three cases that follow trace the FRBR Group 1 entities (WEMI) in resources such as those sitting on a library's physical or digital shelves. The first two cases apply a top-down approach, filtering from work down to items. The third case reverses course, beginning instead with the items.

Case Number One: Poets Twyla Hansen and Linda Hasselstrom prepared a collection of their poems that reflect the influence of the Great Plains. Entitled *Dirt Songs: A Plains Duet*, the book was published in 2011 by the Backwaters Press. The book has not been reprinted or released in other formats. Copies of the 2011 publication are owned by the University of Nebraska–Lincoln Libraries and the Lincoln City Libraries. Figure 1.6 shows a diagram of the FRBR Group 1 entities for *Dirt Songs: A Plains Duet*.

Given that this case includes a single work, a single manifestation, and a single expression, filtering out the aspects of the resource that reflect each level may seem superfluous. However, the example serves as a reminder to mentally separate the content of a resource (the realm of the work and expression) from

Figure 1.5
Attributes and Relationships in an Example Bibliographic Record

		Attributes and relationships for the . . .
Author	Cather, Willa, 1873-1947.	w
Preferred Title	My Ántonia. Spanish	w (preferred title) e (addition of language)
Title	Mi Ántonia / Willa Cather ; traducción de Gema Moral Bartolomé.	m
Edition	Primera edición en DeBols!llo	m
Publisher	Barcelona : Random House Mondadori, 2004.	m
Description	382 pages ; 18 cm.	m
Content Type	Text	e
Media Type	Unmediated	m
Carrier Type	Volume	m
Series	Clásicos ; 57	m
Notes	Translated from the original English.	e
Summary	In the late nineteenth century, a fourteen-year-old immigrant girl from Bohemia and a ten-year-old orphan boy arrive in Black Hawk, Nebraska, and in teaching each other form a friendship that will last a lifetime.	e
Subject	Frontier and pioneer life—Nebraska—Fiction Farmers' spouses—Nebraska—Fiction Women pioneers—Nebraska—Fiction	w
Additional Contributors	Moral Bartolome, Gema, translator.	e
ISBN	9788497931533	m
Call Number	PS3505.A87 M818 2004	i
Local Note	Copy donated by the Nebraska Spanish Language Foundation.	i
	Work (w); Expression (e); Manifestation (m); Item (i)	

the physical form(s) that house the content (the manifestation and item levels).

Case Number Two: Mary Pipher wrote a nonfiction book on caring for aging parents titled *Another Country: Navigating the Emotional Terrain of Our Elders*.

Figure 1.6
FRBR Group 1 Entities for *Dirt Songs: A Plains Duet*

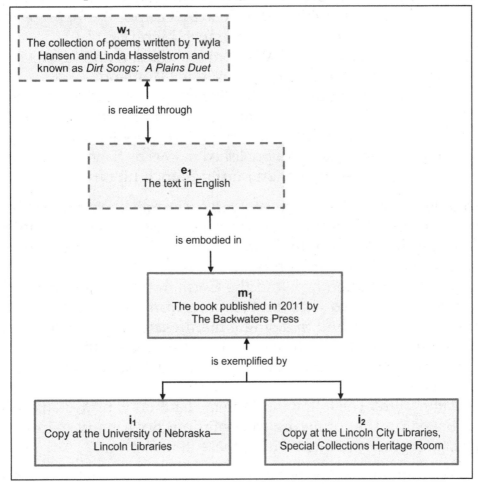

The branches of your library have regular print and large print copies in the original English, as well as translations in Spanish and German. Also, the abridged audiobook in English is available on cassette. Modeling the expressions, manifestations, and items of this work in your collection results in the following outline:

w_1 Mary Pipher's *Another Country: Navigating the Emotional Terrain of Our Elders*

     e_1 the original English text

         m_1 the book published in 1999 by Riverhead

            i_1 Copy at the Gere Branch Library

            i_2 Copy autographed by the author at the Bennett Martin Branch Library, Special Collections

            i_3 Copy at the Anderson Branch Library

         m_2 the large-print book published in 1999 by Wheeler

i_4 Copy at Eiseley Branch Library

e_2 the Spanish translation by Elvira Maldonado

m_3 the book published in 2000 by Grupo

i_5 Copy 1 at the Walt Branch Library

i_6 Copy 2 at the Walt Branch Library, damaged

e_3 the German translation by Susanne Dahmann

m_4 the book published in 2000 by Wolfgang Kruger Verlag

i_7 Copy at the Anderson Branch Library

e_4 spoken word in English, abridged, read by Joan Allen

m_5 the audio cassettes published in 1999 by Simon & Schuster Audio

i_8 Copy at Bennett Martin Branch Library

In this example, Mary Pipher's *Another Country* is a distinct, independent intellectual creation—in FRBR terms, a work. All of the expression, manifestation, and item entities link back to this single work (w_1). Three of the expressions are realized in the form of alpha-numeric notation (the original English text [e_1], the Spanish translation [e_2], and the German translation [e_3]), while the fourth expression is realized via sound (spoken word [e_4]). With one exception, each expression is embodied in a single manifestation. The exception is the original English text (e_1), which has the two manifestations of regular print (m_1) and large print (m_2) editions. Finally, each manifestation is exemplified by one to three items.

Case Number Three: The following 14 items land on your desk (physically or digitally). Based on the following information, how many manifestations, expressions, and works are there within these items?

- Two Spanish translations of Mark Twain's *The Adventures of Tom Sawyer*: one translated by Adolfo de Alba and published in 1971 by Porrúa, and one translated by Celia Filipetto and published in 2002 by Ambrosia.
- Two copies of a book published in 1972 by the World Publishing Company that include the text of *The Adventures of Tom Sawyer*, illustrations by Louis Slobodkin, and an introduction by May Lamberton Becker.
- An electronic reproduction of the first American edition from 1876 of *The Adventures of Tom Sawyer* available in Hathi Trust. Also, a microfilm reproduction of the same edition produced by Research Publications.
- Two CD copies and one cassette copy of an audiobook of *The Adventures of Tom Sawyer* published in 2008 by Blackstone Audio, Inc. William Dufris reads the text.
- One downloadable audiobook of *The Adventures of Tom Sawyer* read by Grover Gardner. Tantor Media produced the audiobook in 2008.
- Two copies of John D. Evans's *A Tom Sawyer Companion*, published in 1993 by University Press of America, Inc.

- One braille book of *The Adventures of Tom Sawyer* published in 1979 by Perfection Form Co.
- One item from special collections: the first American edition of *The Adventures of Tom Sawyer* published in 1876 by the American Publishing Company.

Before looking at Figure 1.7, outline or diagram the works, expressions, and manifestations of these 14 items on your own. As a way to aid the process, try making a notecard for each item. Sort the item notecards into manifestations, group the manifestations into expressions, then tie the expressions to works.

Figure 1.7
FRBR Group 1 Entities for *The Adventures of Tom Sawyer*

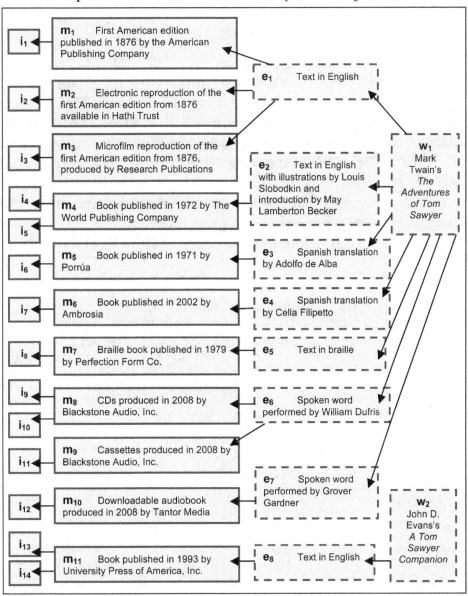

The 14 items on your desk arrange into two works, eight expressions, and 11 manifestations. Mark Twain's *The Adventures of Tom Sawyer* (shown in Figure 1.7 as w_1) is realized through seven expressions: four expressed in alphanumeric notation (e_1, e_2, e_3, e_4), one in braille notation (e_5), and two in spoken word (e_6, e_7). The additions of illustrations and an introduction distinguish e_2 from e_1, while the translators differentiate the two Spanish translations of e_3 and e_4. Likewise, the two spoken word expressions (e_6, e_7) are performed by two different readers. The different forms of carrier divide m_1 (printed book), m_2 (electronic reproduction), and m_3 (microfilm) as well as m_8 (CD) and m_9 (cassette). Finally, John D. Evans's *A Tom Sawyer Companion* (w_2) is realized through one expression (e_8), which is embodied in one manifestation (m_{11}), which is exemplified by two items (i_{13}, i_{14}).

FRBR Group 2 and Group 3 Entities

FRBR defines the Group 1 entities as "products of intellectual or artistic endeavor." Bibliographic records serve as surrogates for these interconnected works, expressions, manifestations, and items. FRBR and FRAD designate two additional, related entity groups (see Figure 1.8). Group 2 entities are the persons, families, and corporate bodies "responsible for the intellectual or artistic content, the physical production and dissemination, or the custodianship of such products." Authors, editors, translators, artists, publishers, printers, and owners belong in this group. Group 3 entities "serve as the subjects of intellectual or artistic endeavor," encompassing concepts, objects, events, and places in addition to all of the entities in Groups 1 and 2 (FRBR 3.1). In other words, a

Figure 1.8
FRBR/FRAD Group 1, Group 2, and Group 3 Entities

Group 1 Entities Products of intellectual or artistic endeavor	Group 2 Entities Those responsible for the intellectual/artistic content, the physical production and dissemination, or the custodianship of Group 1 entities	Group 3 Entities The subjects of intellectual or artistic endeavor
Work (W)		Concept (C)
Expression (E)	Person (P)	Object (O)
Manifestation (M)	Family (F)	Event (Ev)
Item (I)	Corporate body (Cb)	Place (Pl)
		+ Group 1, Group 2

Source: FRBR 3.1

work may have as a subject an entity from Group 1 (WEMI), Group 2 (PFCb), or Group 3 (COEvPl). An author could write a commentary about Mark Twain's *The Adventures of Tom Sawyer* (a Group 1 work), a biography of Mark Twain (a Group 2 person), or a description of the Mississippi River valley (a Group 3 place).

Authority records document attributes of Group 2 and Group 3 entities. Names, dates, and titles serve as attributes of a person (FRBR 4.6), while associated places or numbers characterize corporate bodies (FRBR 4.7). Chapter 3 of this workbook covers authority records in more detail.

The FRBR document (3.2.2, 3.2.9) uses the letter *e* as an abbreviation for both expressions (a Group 1 entity) and events (a Group 3 entity). To clearly distinguish between the two entities, this workbook uses *e* for expressions and *ev* for events.

FRBR Relationships

The relationships between FRBR entities create a tangled network leading from one entity to the next. Many of these relationships have long been implicitly shown in bibliographic records. With FRBR, these relationships become more explicit and defined.

As shown previously in Figure 1.3, the primary relationships between the Group 1 entities tie a hierarchy of works, expressions, manifestations, and items together. A work *is realized through* an expression, and an expression *realizes* a work. Other nonprimary, lateral types of relationships also exist between related Group 1 entities (FRBR 5.3). For example, a work may be an adaptation of another work. Think of all of the movies adapted from books, sometimes with substantial plot or character changes. In those cases, w_1 (the book) *has the adaptation* w_2 (the movie), and w_2 (the movie) *is an adaptation of* w_1 (the book). Two works may also exist in a whole/part relationship: a single monograph (w_1) *is part of* a series (w_2); an essay (w_1) *is part of* an anthology (w_2). One manifestation may be a reproduction of another manifestation: the microfilm of *The Adventures of Tom Sawyer* produced by Research Publications *is a reproduction of* the first American edition published in 1876 by the American Publishing Company. Many other types of nonprimary relationships occur between Group 1 entities. These relationships link the entities together into a family tree of works, expressions, manifestations, and items.

FRBR Group 2 entities (person, family, and corporate body) and Group 3 entities (concept, object, event, and place) also have relationships to Group 1 entities and to each other (FRBR 5.2). Willa Cather (a person) is the creator of *My Ántonia* (a work). Mary Pipher's *Another Country: Navigating the Emotional Terrain of Our Elders* (a work) has as a subject *aging parents* (a concept). As published in 2011 in Omaha, Nebraska, the poetry collection *Dirt Songs: A Plains Duet* (a manifestation) is produced by the Backwaters Press (a corporate body). Samuel Langhorne Clemens (a person) has as an alternate identity Mark Twain (also a person entity). Look back at Figure 1.7; the Group 1 entities there have relationships to authors, illustrators, writers of added commentary, translators, performers, and publishers.

The FRBR-ized Structure of RDA

After working through the FRBR model of entities, attributes, and relationships, the structure and terminology of RDA should seem very familiar (see

Figure 1.9
The Basic Structure of RDA

			FRBR Group
Preliminary materials			
—	—	RDA Table of Contents	
—	(Ch. 0)	Introduction	
Attributes			
Section 1	(Ch. 1–4)	Manifestation and Item (MI)	1
Section 2	(Ch. 5–7)	Work and Expression (WE)	1
Section 3	(Ch. 8–11)	Persons, Families, and Corporate Bodies (PFCb)	2
Section 4	(Ch. 12–16)	Concepts, Objects, Events, and Places (COEvPl)	3
Relationships			
Section 5	(Ch. 17)	Primary relationships between WEMI	1
		Relationships from WEMI to:	
Section 6	(Ch. 18–22)	PFCb	2
Section 7	(Ch. 23)	COEvPl (subjects)	3
		Relationships between:	
Section 8	(Ch. 24–28)	WEMI (related work, related expression, etc.)	1
Section 9	(Ch. 29–32)	PFCb (related place, related family, etc.)	2
Section 10	(Ch. 33–37)	COEvPl (related concept, related object, etc.)	3
Supplementary materials			
Appendices (capitalization, abbreviations, dates, relationship designators, etc.)			
Glossary			
Index			

Figure 1.9). The RDA cataloging guidelines divide into two basic parts: attributes (Sections 1–4) and relationships (Sections 5–10). Supplementary materials at the end consist of appendixes, a glossary, and an index (RDA 0.5). As of this writing, most chapters in RDA Sections 4, 7, and 10—those chapters covering Group 3 entities (COEvPl)—remain undeveloped and are not yet included in the RDA standard.

To navigate within RDA, ask yourself first whether the element you need is an *attribute* describing an entity (proceed to RDA Sections 1–4) or a *relationship* to or between entities (proceed to RDA Sections 5–10). Then consider whether your entity is from Group 1 (WEMI), Group 2 (PFCb), or Group 3 (COEvPl). Work your way down through the RDA sections and chapters until you find what you need. Quick Guides 1.2 and 1.3 provide pathfinders as you learn to navigate RDA.

The RDA Toolkit is the online source for the RDA standard. As of this writing, some resources

Mini-Exercise 1.3
Where in RDA will I find X?

Answer the following questions, using the Quick Guides for Chapter 1 and the RDA table of contents for reference. The RDA table of contents (including instruction numbers) is freely available without a subscription at http://access.rdatoolkit.org. Click on the RDA tab on the left side of the screen. To expand or contract the table of contents, click on the plus (+) or minus (-) sign next to a heading.

In 2006, the U.S. Geological Survey produced a map of the Mark Twain National Forest in Missouri. The map is 58 cm long and 46 cm tall.

1. Dimensions are an element of a(n) _____.

 a) work
 b) expression
 c) manifestation
 d) item

2. The RDA instruction number for *recording dimensions of maps, etc.,* is _____.

David W. Levy's *Mark Twain: The Divided Mind of America's Best-Loved Writer* includes bibliographical references and an index.

3. Supplementary content such as a bibliography or index is an element of a(n) _____.

 a) work
 b) expression
 c) manifestation
 d) item

4. The RDA instruction number for *basic instructions on recording supplementary content* is _____.

The Prince and the Pauper is a novel by Mark Twain.

5. A form such as "novel" is an element of a(n) _____.

 a) work
 b) expression
 c) manifestation
 d) item

6. The RDA instruction number for *basic instructions on recording form* such as "novel" is _____.

such as the RDA table of contents and the Library of Congress–Program for Co-operative Cataloging Policy Statements (LC-PCC PS) are accessible within the Toolkit without a subscription. Online access to the RDA cataloging standard as well as other helpful features requires a subscription. Quick Guide 1.4 highlights the structure, tools, and resources of the RDA Toolkit, and Chapter 4 of this workbook outlines options for purchasing access to the RDA standard through the Toolkit or print editions.

Making the Connection

Connecting people, places, organizations, resources, and concepts in a helpful, meaningful way remains a challenging task. Linking works to expressions, items to manifestations, or a person to a work provides a FRBR-based mechanism for ordering the bibliographic universe. By helping to make these connections, catalogers ultimately link users to the cosmos of information and ideas.

Exercise 1.1

Work, Expression, Manifestation, or Item?

Organize the following resources into works, expressions, manifestations, and items. Construct your answer either in diagram form or in a text outline. Examples of both methods are included in the section "Works, Expressions, Manifestations, and Items in Practice" on page 13 of the workbook.

After completing your diagram or outline, explain the reasons behind your decisions. For instance, why do you consider Resource X a new work and not a new expression of the same work? Some hints as you begin:

Decide if you will take a top-down approach (from works down to items) or instead operate from the bottom up (from items up to works).

Group like things together.

Pay attention to differences like print size, language, or performers.

The following scenario includes 22 items.

Your library has three copies of C. S. Lewis's *The Lion, the Witch, and the Wardrobe* published in 1994 as a paperback book by HarperCollins. The book includes illustrations by Pauline Baynes. Two copies are housed in the Young Adult Fiction Collection, with the third in the Adult Fiction Collection.

Library patrons may access two downloadable audiobooks of *The Lion, the Witch, and the Wardrobe* through the library website. Both are in English and unabridged. Released in 2005 by Harper Audio, one copy is read by Michael York. The other copy is read by a full cast from BBC radio and was released by BBC Audiobooks in 2006.

The young adult librarian hosts a weekly game night at the library. Because the video game *The Chronicles of Narnia: The Lion, the Witch, and the Wardrobe* remains a perennial favorite of the gamers, the library's copy on CD-ROMs remains in the Reserve Collection for in-library use only. Presented by Disney and Walden Media, the interactive multimedia game was released in 2005 by Buena Vista Games.

Last month, the library's book club read *The Lion, the Witch, and the Wardrobe*. Some of the participants prefer large print books, so one copy is now in the Large Print Collection. The book was published in 1987 by Scholastic and includes the illustrations by Pauline Baynes. The book club leader requested a copy of *A Reader's Guide through the Wardrobe: Exploring C. S. Lewis's Classic Story* by Leland Ryken and Marjorie Lamp Mead. Published in 2005 by InterVarsity Press, one copy is now available in the Nonfiction Collection.

Your library includes many Spanish-language materials. HarperCollins published the Spanish translation of *The Lion, the Witch, and the Wardrobe* by Teresa Mlawer in 2002 as both a printed book and an eBook. The Spanish Language Collection houses the printed book, and the eBook is accessible via the library website.

One of the treasures in Special Collections is a specially bound and embellished copy of *The Lion, the Witch, and the Wardrobe* from 1950 published by Geoffrey Bles. This publication had Lewis's original English text with illustrations by Pauline Baynes. Patrons can more easily access a second copy of the same 1950 publication available in the Reserve Collection.

Macmillan published C. S. Lewis's *The Lion, the Witch, and the Wardrobe* in 1950 and included the illustrations by Pauline Baynes. The library has two copies: one in the Adult Fiction Collection and one in Preservation due to a damaged back cover.

Capitalizing on the success of the weekly game night, the young adult librarian organized a showing of the movie *The Chronicles of Narnia: The Lion, the Witch, and the Wardrobe* from Walt Disney Pictures and Walden Media. The library has a Blu-ray player and purchased a copy of the Blu-ray disc distributed by Buena Vista Home Entertainment in 2008. That copy is now available for loan in the Audiovisual Collection. For patrons who do not have a Blu-ray player at home, the Audiovisual Collection also includes two copies of the DVD distributed by Buena Vista Home Entertainment in 2005. In addition, a local film buff donated to Special Collections a set of the movie's film reels and sound discs released in 2005 by Buena Vista Pictures.

The paperbacks of *The Lion, the Witch, and the Wardrobe* in the Young Adult Fiction Collection are showing wear. The acquisitions department procured one copy in a library binding published in 1994 by HarperCollins to add to the worn copies in the Young Adult Fiction Collection. The library binding book includes the illustrations by Pauline Baynes.

Patrons really enjoyed the downloadable audiobook of *The Lion, the Witch, and the Wardrobe* performed by Michael York. However, some library patrons do not have Internet access at home or the equipment needed to listen to a downloadable audiobook. They can now experience Michael York's performance by checking out either the Playaway or CD version. The Audiovisual Collection includes two copies of the CDs, released in 2006 by HarperCollins, and one copy of the Playaway, released in 2007 by Playaway Digital Audio.

Exercise 1.2

Entities, Attributes, and Relationships

Part 1: Entities and Attributes

Label the elements from the following bibliographic record as attributes of a work (w), expression (e), manifestation (m), or item (i).

Author	Dickerson, Matthew T., 1963-, author.	
Title	Narnia and the Fields of Arbol : the environmental vision of C.S. Lewis / Matthew Dickerson and David O'Hara.	1. m
Publisher	Lexington, Kentucky : The University Press of Kentucky, [2009]	2. m
Description	xiii, 304 pages ; 24 cm.	3. m
Content Type	Text	4. e
Media Type	Unmediated	5. m
Carrier Type	Volume	6. m
Series	Culture of the land	7. m
Bibliography	Includes bibliographical references (pages 261-287) and index.	8. e
Summary	Examines The chronicles of Narnia, The great divorce, The abolition of man, the Ransom books, and Lewis's essays and personal correspondence, connecting his writing with that of authors more traditionally associated with environmentalism such as Wendell Berry, Aldo Leopold, and Gary Snyder.	9. e
Contents	Introduction: ecological crisis, environmental critique, and Christian imagination – What he thought about everything – Nature and meaning in the history of Narnia – The magician's nephew: creation and Narnian ecology – The last battle and the end of Narnia – Out of the silent planet: re-imagining ecology – Perelandra: creation and conscience – That hideous strength: assault on the soil and soul of England – The re-enchantment of creation.	
Subject	Lewis, C. S. (Clive Staples), 1898-1963 – Criticism and interpretation. Environmental protection in literature. Environmental policy in literature.	
Additional Contributors	O'Hara, David, 1969-, author.	
ISBN	9780813125220	10. m
Call Number	PR6023.E926 Z6419 2009	11. i
Local Note	Library's copy autographed by the authors.	12. i

Part 2: Entities and Relationships

1. "Dickerson, Matthew T., 1963-" and "O'Hara, David, 1969-" are examples of _____ entities.

   a) Group 1
   (b) Group 2
   c) Group 3

2. Dickerson and O'Hara signed the copy of the book owned by the library. They have a relationship as autographers to the _____ described in the record.

   a) work
   b) expression
   c) manifestation
   (d) item

3. The subjects "Environmental protection in literature" and "Environmental policy in literature" are examples of _____ entities.

   a) Group 1
   b) Group 2
   (c) Group 3

4. The _____ *Narnia and the Fields of Arbol: The Environmental Vision of C. S. Lewis* has as subjects "Lewis, C. S. (Clive Staples), 1898-1963—Criticism and interpretation," "Environmental protection in literature," and "Environmental policy in literature."

   (a) work
   b) expression
   c) manifestation
   d) item

5. The _____ described in the bibliographic record in Part 1 of this exercise was published by the University Press of Kentucky. *(Hint: Which Group 1 entity has the attribute "Publisher"?)*

   a) work
   b) expression
   (c) manifestation
   d) item

From *The RDA Workbook: Learning the Basics of Resource Description and Access.* Margaret Mering, Editor. Santa Barbara, CA: Libraries Unlimited. Copyright © 2014

Exercise 1.3

Navigating the RDA Table of Contents

The scenario: You have been asked to catalog the following resources. Before preparing the records, you would like to read through the relevant RDA instructions. List the RDA instruction numbers pertaining to the attributes (elements) of the resources described.

The RDA table of contents (including instruction numbers) is freely available without a subscription at http://access.rdatoolkit.org. Click on the RDA tab on the left side of the screen. To expand or contract the table of contents, click on the plus (+) or minus (-) sign next to a heading. Consult Figure 1.9 (The Basic Structure of RDA) on page 20 of the workbook and the Quick Guides for Chapter 1 as needed.

Resource A

Thomas Martin edited *Reading the Classics with C. S. Lewis*. The book contains 20 chapters written by various contributors.

Example: The title page of the book includes *Reading the Classics with C. S. Lewis*.
A *title* found on a title page is an element of a(n) _____.

- a) work
- b) expression
- c) manifestation
- d) item

The RDA instruction number for *recording the title proper* is _____.
Answer: c) manifestation   RDA 2.3.2.7

      The path to the answer through the RDA Table of Contents:

    Section 1: Recording attributes of manifestation & item

        Chapter 2: Identifying manifestations and items

            2.3 Title

                2.3.2 Title proper

                    2.3.2.7 Recording the title proper

1. This book has two publishers, Baker Academic and Paternoster Press.
   The *publication statement* is an element of a(n) _____.

   - a) work
   - b) expression
   - c) manifestation
   - d) item

   The RDA instruction number for recording *more than one publisher* is
   2.8.4.5 .

2. The book includes bibliographical references, an index, and a list of Lewis's major critical works.
   Supplementary content such as this is an element of a(n) _____.

   - a) work
   - b) expression

c) manifestation
d) item

The RDA instruction number for *basic instructions on recording supplementary content* is _____.

Resource B

HarperCollins published *The Magician's Nephew* by C. S. Lewis in 2005.

3. This book includes a series statement.
   A *series statement* is an element of a(n) _____.

   a) work
   b) expression
   (c) manifestation
   d) item

   The RDA instruction number for *recording title proper of series* is _____.

4. The book was published in New York.
   The *publication statement* is an element of a(n) _____.

   a) work
   b) expression
   (c) manifestation
   d) item

   The RDA instruction number for *recording place of publication* is _____.

Resource C

In 2009, HarperCollins released *The Magician's Nephew* as an eBook, including the text by C. S. Lewis and illustrations by Pauline Baynes.

5. The content type of this eBook is *text*.
   Content type is an element of a(n) _____.

   form

   a) work
   (b) expression
   c) manifestation
   d) item

   The RDA instruction number for *basic instructions on recording content type* is _____.

6. The media type of this eBook is *computer*.
   Media type is an element of a(n) _____.

   carrier

   a) work
   b) expression
   (c) manifestation
   d) item

   The RDA instruction number for *basic instructions on recording media type* is _____.

7. The carrier type of this eBook is *online resource*.
   Carrier type is an element of a(n) _____.

   a) work
   b) expression
   c) manifestation
   d) item

   The RDA instruction number for *basic instructions on recording carrier type* is _____.

8. The ISBN for the eBook is 9780007319626.
   An *identifier* such as an ISBN is an element of a(n) _____.

   a) work
   b) expression
   c) manifestation
   d) item

   The RDA instruction number for *basic instructions on recording identifiers* such as an ISBN is _____.

9. The extent of this eBook is *1 online resource*.
   Extent is an element of a(n) _____.

   a) work
   b) expression
   c) manifestation
   d) item

   The RDA instruction number for *basic instructions on recording extent* is _____.

Resource D

Gemma Gallart translated into Spanish the novel *Prince Caspian* by C. S. Lewis. In 2008, Rayo published the book, including the illustrations by Pauline Baynes.

10. The book is 20 cm tall.
    Dimensions are an element of a(n) _____.

    a) work
    b) expression
    c) manifestation
    d) item

    The RDA instruction number for *dimensions of carrier – volumes* is _____.

11. Some of Pauline Baynes's illustrations are in color.
    Color content is an element of a(n) _____.

    a) work
    b) expression
    c) manifestation
    d) item

    The RDA instruction number for recording *details of color content* is _____.

12. The title page includes three statements of responsibility (*C. S. Lewis ; traducción de Gemma Gallart ; illustraciones de Pauline Baynes*).

Statement of responsibility is an element of a(n) _____.

   a) work
   b) expression
   (c) manifestation
   d) item

The RDA instruction number for *more than one statement of responsibility* is _____.

13. At your library, this book will have the call number PR6023.E926 P718 2008.
   An *identifier* such as a call number is an element of a(n) _____.

   a) work
   b) expression
   c) manifestation
   (d) item

The RDA instruction number for *basic instructions on recording identifiers* such as a call number is _____.

Resource E

Paper engineer Robert Sabuda and artist Matthew Armstrong created *The Chronicles of Narnia*, a pop-up book based on the books by C. S. Lewis.

14. Due to the fragility of a pop-up book, this resource is recommended for persons over five years of age.
   Intended audience is an element of a(n) _____.

   (a) work
   b) expression
   c) manifestation
   d) item

The RDA instruction number for *basic instructions on recording the intended audience* is _____.

15. You would like to include a brief summary of the content of this pop-up book.
   Summarization of the content is an element of a(n) _____.

   a) work
   (b) expression
   c) manifestation
   d) item

The RDA instruction number for *basic instructions on summarizing the content* is _____.

16. This copy of the pop-up book will be noncirculating and restricted to library use only.
   For this copy of the pop-up book, *restrictions on use* is an element of a(n) _____.

   a) work
   b) expression
   c) manifestation
   (d) item

The RDA instruction number for *basic instructions on recording restrictions on use* is _____.

From *The RDA Workbook: Learning the Basics of Resource Description and Access.*
Margaret Mering, Editor. Santa Barbara, CA: Libraries Unlimited. Copyright © 2014

Resource F

A seventh-grade class from the local middle school wrote and illustrated short stories incorporating the characters from *The Chronicles of Narnia*. The stories were gathered and bound into a book.

17. This book was issued in an unpublished form—it was produced and bound at the local middle school.
    A *production statement* for an unpublished resource is an element of a(n) _____.

    a) work
    b) expression
    c) manifestation
    d) item

    The RDA instruction number for *basic instructions on recording production statements* is _____.

Resource G

Walt Disney Records released a CD in 2008 of the soundtrack of the movie *Prince Caspian*.

18. The container shows a title that differs from the one you transcribed as the title proper.
    A *title* such as the one shown on the container is an element of a(n) _____.

    a) work
    b) expression
    c) manifestation
    d) item

    The RDA instruction number for *recording variant titles* is _____.

19. You consider some of the musical performers significant enough to mention in the bibliographic record.
    Performers, narrators, and/or presenters are an element of a(n) _____.

    a) work
    b) expression
    c) manifestation
    d) item

    The RDA instruction number for *basic instructions on recording performers, narrators, and/or presenters* is _____.

Resource H

BBC Television and WonderWorks produced a television adaptation of *The Chronicles of Narnia*. The program was released as a DVD set.

20. The form of this resource is *television program*.
    A form such as *television program* is an element of a(n) _____.

    a) work
    b) expression
    c) manifestation
    d) item

    The RDA instruction number for *basic instructions on recording form* such as this is _____.

Quick Guide to FRBR/FRAD Attributes and RDA Elements of Group 1 Entities

Selected attributes and elements of works, expressions, manifestations, and items

Group 1 Entity	FRBR/FRAD Attributes	RDA Elements *RDA core element
Work(w)	Title of the work	Title of the work*
	Form of work (examples: novel, play, map)	Form of work*
	Date of the work	Date of work*
	Context for the work (FRBR), History (FRAD)	History of the work
	Place of origin of the work	Place of origin of the work*
	Other distinguishing characteristic	Other distinguishing characteristic of the work*
		Signatory to a treaty, etc.*
	Intended audience	Intended audience
	Intended termination	
	Identifier for the work	Identifier for the work*
	For musical works: medium of performance numeric designation key	For musical works: medium of performance* numeric designation of a musical work* key*
	For cartographic works: coordinates equinox	For cartographic works: coordinates equinox
Expression(e)	Title of the expression	—
	Form of expression (examples: alpha-numeric notation, musical notation, spoken word, photographic image, etc.)	Content type* (examples: text, notated music, spoken word, still image, etc.)
	Language of expression	Language of expression* Language of the content

From *The RDA Workbook: Learning the Basics of Resource Description and Access*.
Margaret Mering, Editor. Santa Barbara, CA: Libraries Unlimited. Copyright © 2014

Group 1 Entity	FRBR/FRAD Attributes	RDA Elements *RDA core element
	Date of expression	Date of expression*
	Extent of the expression (examples: number of words in a text, playing time)	Duration
	Other distinguishing characteristic	Other distinguishing characteristic of the expression*
	Identifier for the expression	Identifier for the expression*
	Summarization of content	Summarization of the content
	—	Supplementary content (examples: index, bibliography, introduction)
	—	Illustrative content
	Color content	Color content
	—	Artistic and/or technical credits
	—	Performer, narrator, and/or presenter
	Critical response to the expression	Award
	For cartographic image/object: scale	Scale*
Manifestation (m)	Title of the manifestation	Title*
	Statement of responsibility	Statement of responsibility*
	Edition/issue designation	Edition statement*
	Place of publication/distribution	Production statement*
	Publisher/distributor	Publication statement*
	Date of publication/distribution	Distribution statement*
	Fabricator/manufacturer	Manufacture statement*
		Copyright date*
	Series statement	Series statement*
	—	Media type (examples: video, audio, computer, unmediated)

Group 1 Entity	FRBR/FRAD Attributes		RDA Elements *RDA core element
Manifestation (or)	Form of carrier		Carrier type* (examples: videodisc, online resource, volume)
	Extent of the carrier		Extent*
	Dimensions of the carrier		Dimensions
	Manifestation identifier (examples: ISBN, ISSN)		Identifier for the manifestation*
	Terms of availability ✱ circulation?		Terms of availability
	Access restrictions on the manifestation		Restrictions on use / Restrictions on access
	Access address (remote access electronic resource)		Uniform resource locator
	—		Note
	—		Preferred citation
	—		Sound characteristic
	—		Digital file characteristic
	—		Video characteristic
	For serials: numbering		Numbering of serials*
Item(i)	Item identifier (examples: bar code, RFID tag, call number)		Identifier for the item
	Provenance of the item		Custodial history of item / Immediate source of acquisition of item
	Exhibition history		—
	Condition of the item / Marks/inscriptions		Item-specific carrier characteristic
	Access restrictions on the item		Restrictions on use / Restrictions on access
	—		Note
	—		Uniform resource locator

Quick Guide 1.2
Quick Guide to RDA
Which RDA chapter do I need?

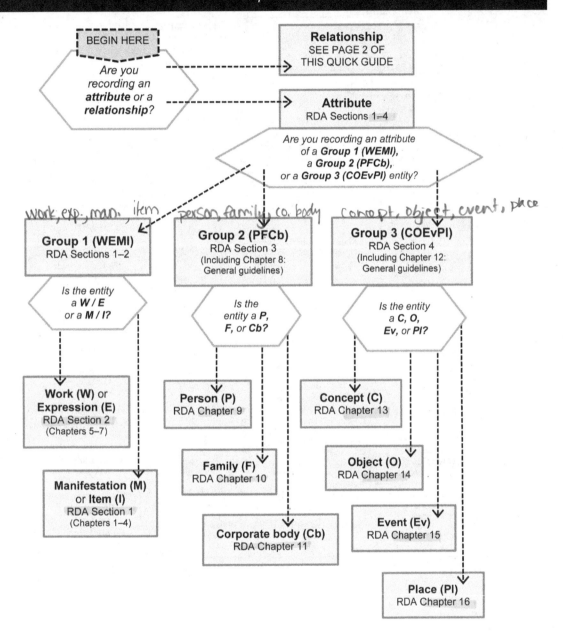

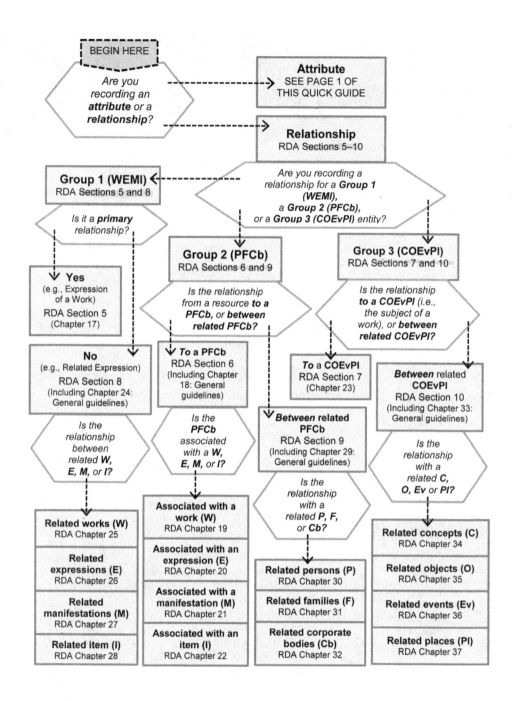

Quick Guide 1.3
Quick Guide to WEMI Attributes

Where can I find the RDA guidelines for a particular WEMI attribute?

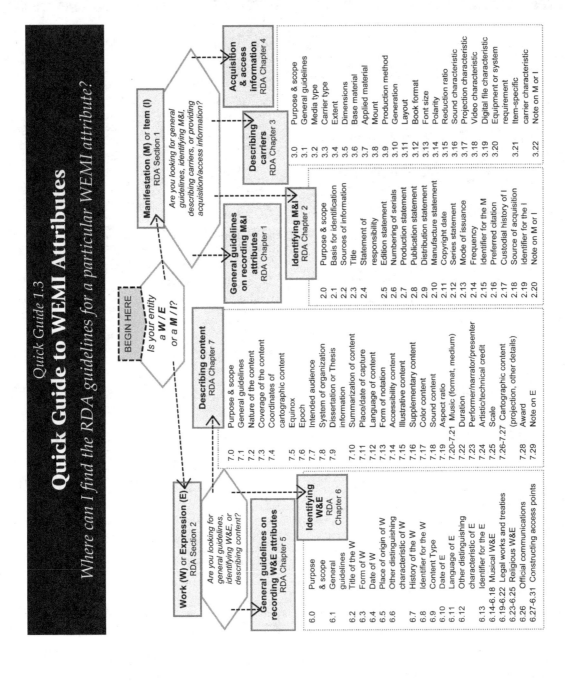

BEGIN HERE

*Is your entity a **W / E** or a **M / I**?*

Work (W) or Expression (E)
RDA Section 2

Are you looking for general guidelines, identifying W&E, or describing content?

General guidelines on recording W&E attributes
RDA Chapter 5

6.0	Purpose & scope
6.1	General guidelines
6.2	Title of the W
6.3	Form of W
6.4	Date of W
6.5	Place of origin of W
6.6	Other distinguishing characteristic of W
6.7	History of the W
6.8	Identifier for the W
6.9	Content Type
6.10	Date of E
6.11	Language of E
6.12	Other distinguishing characteristic of E
6.13	Identifier for the E
6.14-6.18	Musical W&E
6.19-6.22	Legal works and treaties
6.23-6.25	Religious W&E
6.26	Official communications
6.27-6.31	Constructing access points

Identifying W&E
RDA Chapter 6

Describing content
RDA Chapter 7

7.0	Purpose & scope
7.1	General guidelines
7.2	Nature of the content
7.3	Coverage of the content
7.4	Coordinates of cartographic content
7.5	Equinox
7.6	Epoch
7.7	Intended audience
7.8	System of organization
7.9	Dissertation or Thesis information
7.10	Summarization of content
7.11	Place/date of capture
7.12	Language of content
7.13	Form of notation
7.14	Accessibility content
7.15	Illustrative content
7.16	Supplementary content
7.17	Color content
7.18	Sound content
7.19	Aspect ratio
7.20-7.21	Music (format, medium)
7.22	Duration
7.23	Performer/narrator/presenter
7.24	Artistic/technical credit
7.25	Scale
7.26-7.27	Cartographic content (projection, other details)
7.28	Award
7.29	Note on E

Manifestation (M) or Item (I)
RDA Section 1

Are you looking for general guidelines, identifying M&I, describing carriers, or providing acquisition/access information?

General guidelines on recording M&I attributes
RDA Chapter 1

Identifying M&I
RDA Chapter 2

2.0	Purpose & scope
2.1	Basis for identification
2.2	Sources of information
2.3	Title
2.4	Statement of responsibility
2.5	Edition statement
2.6	Numbering of serials
2.7	Production statement
2.8	Publication statement
2.9	Distribution statement
2.10	Manufacture statement
2.11	Copyright date
2.12	Series statement
2.13	Mode of issuance
2.14	Frequency
2.15	Identifier for the M
2.16	Preferred citation
2.17	Custodial history of I
2.18	Source of acquisition
2.19	Identifier for the I
2.20	Note on M or I

Describing carriers
RDA Chapter 3

3.0	Purpose & scope
3.1	General guidelines
3.2	Media type
3.3	Carrier type
3.4	Extent
3.5	Dimensions
3.6	Base material
3.7	Applied material
3.8	Mount
3.9	Production method
3.10	Generation
3.11	Layout
3.12	Book format
3.13	Font size
3.14	Polarity
3.15	Reduction ratio
3.16	Sound characteristic
3.17	Projection characteristic
3.18	Video characteristic
3.19	Digital file characteristic
3.20	Equipment or system requirement
3.21	Item-specific carrier characteristic
3.22	Note on M or I

Acquisition & access information
RDA Chapter 4

Quick Guide to the RDA Toolkit
Utilizing the Toolkit, an online resource for the RDA standard and more
www.rdatoolkit.org

RDA tab	Tools tab		Resources tab
For the essential tool of the trade – the RDA standard	*For the RDA power tools in your toolbox*		*For tools that supplement and refine RDA*

✖ RDA Table of contents*

Expandable, collapsible online version in the column at the left of the screen.

Printed version available by clicking on *RDA Table of Contents* then the printer icon.

✖ RDA instructions

The content of the RDA standard. Includes hyperlinks to related RDA instructions and LC-PCC Policy Statements.

✖ RDA Update History

Previous versions of the RDA instructions.

✖ RDA: Element Set

An alternative view of the RDA content that pulls together related definitions and instructions. A good bridge tool to learning RDA.

✖ RDA Mappings*

Crosswalks showing corresponding elements between two data sets, such as the MARC Bibliographic to RDA Mapping.

✖ Examples of RDA Records (JSC)*

A link to full MARC record examples of RDA cataloging developed by the Joint Steering Committee for Development of RDA (JSC).

✖ Workflows

A place for user-created documents such as cataloging procedures for specific formats. Workflows can be set for either global or local access. Check out the global workflows to see how other institutions are putting RDA into practice.

✖ Maps

Crosswalks such as those in the RDA Mappings, but user-created. Maps can be set for either global or local access.

✖ Entity Relationship Diagram (ERD)

Visual diagrams of the FRBR and FRAD entities, attributes, and relationships.

✖ Schemas*

Machine-readable, downloadable RDA schemas.

✖ AACR2

The text of the *Anglo-American Cataloging Rules*, Second Edition.

✖ Library of Congress–Program for Cooperative Cataloging Policy Statements (LC-PCC PS)*

Details of LC/PCC practice and pre-cataloging decisions concerning RDA.

✖ Other Resources*

Links to other online resources (mostly open access) such as the Dublin Core Metadata Initiative and the Open Metadata Registry.

*open access content as of May 2013

How do I...	...search the RDA Toolkit?	For quick searching of RDA content, use the *RDA Quick Search* box in the toolbar. Type in an RDA instruction number or RDA term.
		For advanced searching of RDA plus other content, click on the *advanced search* icon (the magnifying glass). Enter a phrase or string to search, select documents to search, or limit your search by AACR2 rule number or RDA instruction type.
	...customize the RDA Toolkit?	Set up a user profile by clicking on the *create profile* icon (the person with the blue cross). Here you can customize the Toolkit settings and access saved searches, bookmarks, workflows, and maps.
	...view only the core instructions in the RDA Toolkit?	After opening content from the *RDA* tab, click on the *view text* icon (the multi-colored page with a magnifying glass). Filter by core element instructions or by basic instructions. The basic instructions include the core elements plus a few more.
	...see how other libraries are using RDA and the RDA Toolkit?	Look at the global workflows and maps available in the Tools tab. They provide a wealth of information on how other institutions are cataloging with RDA. If you decide to create a local workflow, consider using one of the global workflows as a starting point.
	...learn more about the RDA Toolkit?	The RDA Toolkit website (www.rdatoolkit.org) includes many freely available resources for learning about the Toolkit. Check out the resources listed in the *Navigation* panel on the left side of the screen, especially the blog and the teaching & training section. Register for the RDA Toolkit Essentials webinar or view an archived recording.

RDA Toolkit. Chicago: American Library Association; Ottawa: Canadian Library Association; London: Chartered Institute of Library and Information Professionals (CILIP), 2010-. http://www.rdatoolkit.org/ (cited May 9, 2013).

From *The RDA Workbook: Learning the Basics of Resource Description and Access.*
Margaret Mering, Editor. Santa Barbara, CA: Libraries Unlimited. Copyright © 2014

2

RDA in the Real World: Preparing Bibliographic Records

Corinne Jacox, Margaret Mering, Melissa Moll, Emily Dust Nimsakont, and Deirdre Routt

A copy of *The Literacy Cookbook* by Sarah Tantillo sits on your desk. The library already has multiple hold requests from patrons wanting to read this guide on effective literacy education. Your task is to catalog the book and rush it to the first patron in line. Opening the book's cover, you find that the title page reads *The Literacy Cookbook A PRACTICAL GUIDE TO EFFECTIVE READING, WRITING, SPEAKING, AND LISTENING INSTRUCTION*—with this exact mixture of upper- and lowercase letters. The title page verso shows a place of publication of *San Francisco, CA* and includes the statement *First Edition.* How do you take these kernels of information and catalog the book using *Resource Description and Access* (RDA)? What is the process, what are the options to consider, and what else do you need to know?

Chapter 1 of this workbook covered *Functional Requirements for Bibliographic Records* (FRBR), the theoretical underpinning of RDA. This chapter shifts from theory to practice, focusing on the process of cataloging resources. After outlining essential highlights of RDA, the chapter builds a bibliographic record for *The Literacy Cookbook*, a simple printed book.

Goals for Chapter 2:
- Understand the highlights of RDA and compare with *Anglo-American Cataloguing Rules*, Second Edition (AACR2).
- Build on an understanding of FRBR as it relates to RDA.
- Create an RDA record for a simple book.
- Examine examples of RDA records.

Figure 2.1
RDA Highlights

1	How to Spot an RDA Record
2	Elements—*Core*, *Core-if*, and *Core-for-you*
3	*Take What You See:* The Principle of Representation
4	*Transcribe* Versus *Record*
5	Abbreviations (or lack thereof)
6	Terminology—AACR2 Versus RDA
7	Production, Publication, Distribution, Manufacture, and Copyright Date—MARC Field 264
8	Expanding Access within Bibliographic Records
9	Content Type, Media Type, and Carrier Type—The 33x Fields
10	RDA for Content but not Display

RDA Highlights: Ten Points You Should Know

Highlight 1: How to Spot an RDA Record

When searching for an RDA record prepared by an English-language cataloging agency, look for the following data in subfields $b and $e of MARC field 040:

040 _ _ $a ### $b eng $e rda $c ###

Field 040 documents the cataloging source(s) of a record. The language code in subfield $b comes from the *MARC Code List for Languages*. The code *eng* designates the English language. Subfield $e records the description conventions used in the bibliographic record—in this case, RDA.

The *descriptive cataloging form* (or *Desc*) offers a second way to pinpoint most RDA records. Bibliographic records prepared under AACR2 showed the letter *a* for descriptive cataloging form, which comprises character position eighteen of the MARC leader. RDA records that include ISBD punctuation use the letter *i* here instead.

Highlight 2: Elements—Core, Core-if, and Core-for-you

In RDA, an element is "a word, character, or group of words and/or characters representing a distinct unit of bibliographic information" (RDA Glossary). These small precise pieces of data become the building blocks to construct a record. Some elements are required in RDA, while others are required for certain situations. Individual cataloging agencies (such as the Library of Congress

[LC] or your own library) and joint cataloging efforts (such as the Program for Cooperative Cataloging [PCC]) may require additional elements for their own local practices.

The RDA instructions declare some elements as *core* (RDA 0.6.1). These elements provide the nucleus of a bibliographic record, becoming the required, essential bits of information that allow users to find, identify, and select resources. For instance, users need to know the *title proper*—a core element of manifestations—to identify a particular book or DVD. Quick Guides 1.1 and 2.1 list the RDA core elements.

RDA designates other elements as *core-if*. These elements are considered core in RDA *only if* a particular situation applies. For example, the place of distribution becomes core only if a bibliographic record lacks a place of publication (RDA 2.9). The core-if elements provide a second tier of data, supporting user tasks in situations where the first, core tier of information is not available.

The RDA guidelines allow more opportunities for variation in local practices and cataloger's judgment than was permissible under AACR2. Individual institutions may decide that certain elements not considered core in RDA are in fact essential to help their own users identify and select materials. For example, *title proper* is an RDA core element, while *other title information* (such as a subtitle) remains optional. Your library may decide to follow LC-PCC practice for recording other title information, or you could create your own local policy. Chapter 4 of this workbook discusses these local decisions in more detail. When preparing bibliographic records in RDA, remember that some elements are RDA core, some are RDA core-if, some are considered core in LC-PCC guidelines, and others may be local core—in other words, *core-for-you* (see Figure 2.2).

Figure 2.2
Levels of Elements from RDA Core to Local Core

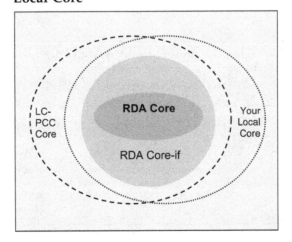

Highlight 3: Take What You See: The Principle of Representation

Reflecting the IFLA *Statement of International Cataloguing Principles* (see Figure 1.1), RDA adopts the principle of representation as a main tenet—a *take what you see and accept what you get* approach (RDA 0.4.3.4). How a resource or entity describes or names itself becomes an important factor when cataloging. What data is included on a title page, title page verso, or title screen? How is that data stated, presented, or formatted? What name does a person or corporate body prefer? The remaining highlights, examples, and workflows in this chapter demonstrate many situations in which to ask such questions and apply the principle of representation—*take what you see, accept what you get.*

Highlight 4: Transcribe versus Record

Some RDA elements are *transcribed* from the source in hand, while others are *recorded*. Transcription puts the principle of representation into practice. With possible exceptions such as capitalization and punctuation, transcribed elements match exactly what is on the piece in hand (RDA 1.7). Title, edition statement, place of publication, and publisher's name are examples of transcribed elements in RDA. Consider a book whose title page verso shows a publisher's name and location as *The Backwaters Press, Omaha, Nebraska*. When recording this information, AACR2 instructed catalogers to disregard the article *the* and to use an abbreviation for *Nebraska* (AACR2 1.4C3, 1.4D2). Under RDA, a cataloger instead transcribes these two elements as shown on the source (RDA 2.8.1.4; see Figure 2.3).

Recorded elements document data about a resource but are not directly transcribed from the source. For instance, a cataloger records the frequency of a newspaper or the number of pages and height of a monograph. The RDA instructions specify which elements are transcribed and which are recorded (see Quick Guide 2.1).

Figure 2.3
Comparison of Recorded and Transcribed Data in AACR2 and RDA

Publisher's Name and Location		
On source:	**AACR2 (recorded)**	**RDA (transcribed)**
The Backwaters Press Omaha, Nebraska	Omaha, Neb. : Backwaters Press	Omaha, Nebraska : The Backwaters Press
The Backwaters Press Omaha, NE	Omaha, NE : Backwaters Press	Omaha, NE : The Backwaters Press

Highlight 5: Abbreviations (or lack thereof)

In comparison to AACR2, RDA instructs catalogers to use fewer abbreviations in bibliographic records. RDA also eliminates Latin abbreviations used in AACR2 such as *S.l.* (*sine loco*) and *s.n.* (*sine nomine*) for an unknown place of publication and name of publisher. As users may be unfamiliar with these abbreviations, RDA instead prefers unabbreviated phrases in the language of the cataloging agency such as *Place of publication not identified* (RDA 2.8.2.6).

Using fewer abbreviations in bibliographic records also reflects the *take what you see* approach to transcription. If a word is spelled out on the source of information, a transcribed field also spells out the word; if abbreviated on the source, the transcription likewise abbreviates. As one example, the edition statement is now a transcribed field under RDA and is thus included in the bibliographic record exactly how it appears on the item (RDA 2.5.1.4). In contrast, AACR2 specified to always abbreviate the word *edition* to *ed.*, regardless of what appeared on the source (AACR2 1.2B1; see Figure 2.4).

Even when RDA elements are recorded rather than transcribed, abbreviations are used much less frequently in RDA than in AACR2. For instance, words such as *pages* or *volumes* are spelled out when recording the extent of a manifestation, rather than abbreviated as *p.* and *v.*, respectively (RDA 3.4.5). Similarly, the word *illustrations* replaces the AACR2 abbreviation *ill.* (RDA 7.15.1.3). Other words used to describe illustrative content in RDA are spelled out accordingly. However, RDA records retain some abbreviations such as *hr.* for *hour(s)*, *min.* for *minute(s)*, and *sec.* for *second(s)* (RDA 7.22.1.3).

Figure 2.4
Comparison of Abbreviations in AACR2 and RDA

Edition Statement		
On source:	**AACR2 (recorded)**	**RDA (transcribed)**
1st edition	1st ed.	1st edition
Second edition	2nd ed.	Second edition
3rd ed.	3rd ed.	3rd ed.
Illustrative Content		
Resource	**AACR2 (recorded)**	**RDA (recorded)**
A book with 300 pages, including illustrations (some in color) and portraits	300 p.	300 pages
	ill. (some col.), ports.	illustrations (some color), portraits

Figure 2.5
Terminology Changes from AACR2 to RDA

AACR2	RDA
Heading	Authorized access point
See reference	Variant access point
See also reference	Authorized access point for related entity
Physical description	Carrier Type
General material designation (GMD)	Content Type, Media Type, Carrier Type
Chief source	Preferred source
Main entry	Preferred title + Authorized access point for creator (if appropriate)
Uniform title	Preferred title (+ other information to differentiate), Conventional collective title

Highlight 6: Terminology—AACR2 versus RDA

For catalogers used to AACR2, part of the RDA learning curve includes changes in terminology. *Headings* in AACR2 become *authorized access points* in RDA, and *uniform titles* shift to *preferred titles*. Figure 2.5 shows some main vocabulary changes.

Highlight 7: Production, Publication, Distribution, Manufacture, and Copyright Date—MARC Field 264

A single resource could be published by one entity, distributed by a second entity, and manufactured by a third. A cataloger could receive an unpublished resource, perhaps a locally produced zine or video recording. A copyright date could differ from the date of publication and provide a critical detail needed to distinguish and identify a particular resource. MARC field 264 encodes and compartmentalizes imprint information such as this, differentiating production, publication, distribution, manufacture, and copyright data. This field is repeatable, with the second indicator distinguishing the function or role of the entity (see Figure 2.6). Guidelines for PCC institutions indicate to use MARC field 264 instead of field 260 for new RDA records (Program for Cooperative Cataloging 2012).

The RDA instructions designate some elements of production, publication, distribution, manufacture, and copyright statements as core. Other elements are core-if in RDA, while still others remain optional. For bibliographic records of published resources, the place of publication, the publisher's name, and the date of publication are all core elements (RDA 2.8). For records of unpublished

Figure 2.6
Distinguishing Function in MARC Field 264

MARC Field 264	
Second Indicator	**Function of entity**
0	Production
1	Publication
2	Distribution
3	Manufacture
4	Copyright notice date

resources, only the date of production is considered core; catalogers may choose to include other optional elements such as place of production (RDA 2.7). Copyright date is an RDA core-if element, becoming core only if a record includes neither the date of publication nor the date of distribution (RDA 2.11).

In RDA, *place of publication* is a transcribed, core element. Sometimes a source of information lists more than one place associated with a particular publisher. RDA requires the first recorded place to be included in a bibliographic record, but a cataloger may choose to include the additional places as well (RDA 2.8.2). In contrast, AACR2 rules required catalogers to record the first-named place, plus "any place given prominence" on the source, plus a place in the home country of the cataloging agency if the other places recorded were not. The record omitted any additional places (AACR2 1.4C5). In RDA, catalogers may transcribe the first place of publication—regardless of whether that place lies in the United States or Canada or England or China—and stop there.

Highlight 8: Expanding Access within Bibliographic Records

Within bibliographic records, RDA offers possibilities to provide more access to and more information about the entities associated with a resource, especially through the statement of responsibility, additional added access points, and relationship designators. The statement of responsibility is a transcribed, core element of manifestations (RDA 2.4). Under RDA, if 14 people authored a resource, a cataloger may transcribe all 14 names in the statement of responsibility. The *rule of three* from AACR2, limiting the number of names to three (AACR2 1.1F5), no longer applies. But perhaps a cataloger or local cataloging agency does not wish to transcribe and type out all 14 names. RDA contains an option to abridge the statement of responsibility, provided that the bibliographic record retains all "essential information" and includes at least the first-named entity (RDA 2.4.1.4; see Figure 2.7). However, including more

Figure 2.7
Comparison of Statements of Responsibility in AACR2 and RDA

Statement of Responsibility (MARC field 245, subfield $c)	
On title page of book:	Reuven Feuerstein, Louis H. Falik, Refael S. Feuerstein, & Krisztina Bohács *Foreword by Yvette Jackson*
AACR2	Reuven Feuerstein . . . [et al.] ; foreword by Yvette Jackson.
RDA	Reuven Feuerstein, Louis H. Falik, Refael S. Feuerstein, & Krisztina Bohács ; foreword by Yvette Jackson. OR Reuven Feuerstein, Louis H. Falik, Refael S. Feuerstein, & Krisztina Bohács. OR Reuven Feuerstein [and three others].

entities in the statement of responsibility and the corresponding added access points (MARC 7xx fields) can assist discovery by catalog users. If a patron searches for all of the resources by Person Thirteen, but the statement of responsibility for this resource includes only the name of Person One, their search results remain incomplete.

Some sources show more than one statement of responsibility—perhaps one person wrote a book, another illustrated it, and a third provided the translation. RDA designates the first *statement of responsibility relating to the title proper* as a required, core element. Additional statements of responsibility remain optional (RDA 2.4.2). The example in Figure 2.7 shows a title page naming four authors of a book plus one author of a foreword to the book—two statements of responsibility. RDA allows the transcription of both statements of responsibility in their entirety; optionally, catalogers may exercise the options to transcribe only the first statement of responsibility or to abridge the statement to the first name only.

Relationship designators (see Figure 2.8) explain the connections between a Group 1 entity (work, expression, manifestation, or item) and a Group 2 entity (person, family, or corporate body). A person could be the *author* or *compiler* of a work (RDA I.2.1); the *illustrator* or *performer* of an expression (RDA I.3.1); the *engraver* of a manifestation (RDA I.4.1); or the *annotator* of an item (RDA I.5.2). A family could be the *former owner* or the *dedicatee* of an item (RDA I.5). A corporate body could be the *degree granting institution* or *sponsoring body* of a work (RDA I.2.2). RDA Appendix I includes an open list of relationship designator terms. The *MARC Code List for Relators* offers a more extensive, controlled vocabulary of relator terms and their equivalent relator codes. MARC fields for main or added entries of personal names (fields 100 and 700) and corporate

Figure 2.8
Examples of Relationship Designators

RDA	RDA in MARC
Borglum, Gutzon, 1867-1941, sculptor.	100 1_ $a Borglum, Gutzon, $d 1867-1941, $e sculptor.
Adams, Ansel, 1902-1984, photographer.	100 1_ $a Adams, Ansel, $d 1902-1984, $e photographer.
Disney, Walt, 1901-1966, animator.	700 1_ $a Disney, Walt, $d 1901-1966, $e animator.
Wiegand, Wayne A., 1946- editor.	700 1_ $a Wiegand, Wayne A., $d 1946- $e editor.
Tedeschi, Anne, translator.	700 1_ $a Tedeschi, Anne, $e translator.
Walczak, Jim, printer.	700 1_ $a Walczak, Jim, $e printer.
Nebraska Educational Television Network, broadcaster.	710 2_ $a Nebraska Educational Television Network, $e broadcaster.

names (fields 110 and 710) include subfields for relator terms ($e) and relator codes ($4).

Highlight 9: Content Type, Media Type, and Carrier Type—The 33x Fields

A CD-ROM and a music CD land in your cataloging in-box. The CD-ROM contains a computer program, and the music CD transmits performed music. To access the content on these two CDs, you need some type of intermediating technological device like a computer (for the CD-ROM) or an audio player (for the music CD). Both the CD-ROM and the music CD are physical discs that digitally convey the content of the resource. In RDA terms, the *computer program* on the CD-ROM and the *performed music* on the music CD are *content types*. A *computer* and an *audio* device are *media types*. Finally, a *computer disc* and an *audio disc* provide two examples of *carrier types*.

These three RDA elements—content type, media type, and carrier type—replace the general material designation (GMD), a term used in AACR2 to indicate "the broad class of material to which an item belongs" (AACR2 Glossary). Some of these broad classes were too general. The GMD *videorecording*, for instance, applied to both VHS tapes and DVDs. The GMD vocabulary also included a mixture of content terms, media terms, and carrier terms. *Cartographic material* and *motion picture* described the content of a resource, while *microscope slide* and *transparency* designated carrier types. Under AACR2, catalogers were forced to choose a single aspect to highlight in the GMD within the title statement (MARC field 245, subfield $h). For resources such as a downloadable video—both an *electronic resource* and a *videorecording*—either choice left out an essential component from the GMD. An RDA record for a downloadable video instead separates the type of content (*two-dimensional moving image*), the type of carrier that houses the content (*online resource*), and the type of media or device needed to access the content on the carrier (a *computer*).

Content type, an expression-level element, is the most abstract way of sorting resources. RDA defines content type as "a categorization reflecting the fundamental form of communication in which the content is expressed and the human sense through which it is intended to be perceived" (RDA 6.9.1.1). Is the content of a given resource communicated via *text* and perceived through sight? Or perhaps the content is communicated via *spoken word* and perceived through hearing? Content type does not depend on physical format. Expressions with the content type *text* could be manifested in the forms of a printed book, an eBook, a microfilm reel, an overhead transparency, or even a PDF file.

Media type and carrier type are elements of manifestations. Media type classifies resources according to the general category of equipment—or "intermediation device"—needed to access the content (RDA 3.2.1.1). Examples of RDA media types include *audio, computer, video,* and *projected.* Some *unmediated* resources like printed books do not require any additional device beyond the resource itself. Carrier type reflects the more specific "format of the storage medium" (RDA 3.3.1.1). The content of a motion picture (a *two-dimensional moving image*) could be carried or stored as a *film reel,* a *videocassette,* a *videodisc,* or an *online resource.* These carrier types are subtypes of media terms. A film reel is an example of a *projected* image carrier, videocassettes and videodiscs are *video* carriers, and online resources belong to the category of *computer* carriers. To view the content of the motion picture, users wind the film reel (the carrier) through the projector (a type of media), insert the DVD into a DVD player, or access the downloadable online resource through a computer.

RDA terms for content type, media type, and carrier type come from predetermined, closed vocabularies found in the RDA standard (RDA 6.9.1.3, 3.2.1.3, 3.3.1.3). Lists of these RDA terms and their corresponding MARC codes are also available on the Library of Congress website as part of the *Value Lists for Codes and Controlled Vocabularies.* MARC fields 336, 337, and 338 encode content type, media type, and carrier type, respectively. In these three fields, subfield $a records terms, while subfield $b records the corresponding MARC codes. RDA bibliographic records may include either one or both of these subfields. Subfield $2 specifies the controlled vocabulary from which the term or code derives. In Figures 2.9 and 2.10, all of the terms come from the RDA vocabularies for content type, media type, or carrier type. Subfield $2 thus records *rdacontent, rdamedia,* or *rdacarrier.*

Figure 2.9

Content Type, Media Type, and Carrier Type for Common Formats

Format	Content Type (MARC field 336)	Media Type (MARC field 337)	Carrier Type (MARC field 338)	RDA in MARC
Print book	text	unmediated	volume	336 _ _ $a text $2 rdacontent 337 _ _ $a unmediated $2 rdamedia 338 _ _ $a volume $2 rdacarrier
eBook	text	computer	online resource	336 _ _ $a text $2 rdacontent 337 _ _ $a computer $2 rdamedia 338 _ _ $a online resource $2 rdacarrier
Audiobook on CD	spoken word	audio	audio disc	336 _ _ $a spoken word $2 rdacontent 337 _ _ $a audio $2 rdamedia 338 _ _ $a audio disc $2 rdacarrier
Downloadable audiobook	spoken word	computer	online resource	336 _ _ $a spoken word $2 rdacontent 337 _ _ $a computer $2 rdamedia 338 _ _ $a online resource $2 rdacarrier
CD-ROM	computer program	computer	computer disc	336 _ _ $a computer program $2 rdacontent 337 _ _ $a computer $2 rdamedia 338 _ _ $a computer disc $2 rdacarrier
Music CD	performed music	audio	audio disc	336 _ _ $a performed music $2 rdacontent 337 _ _ $a audio $2 rdamedia 338 _ _ $a audio disc $2 rdacarrier
DVD	two-dimensional moving image	video	videodisc	336 _ _ $a two-dimensional moving image $2 rdacontent 337 _ _ $a video $2 rdamedia 338 _ _ $a videodisc $2 rdacarrier
Downloadable video	two-dimensional moving image	computer	online resource	336 _ _ $a two-dimensional moving image $2 rdacontent 337 _ _ $a computer $2 rdamedia 338 _ _ $a online resource $2 rdacarrier

Figure 2.10
Example of a Resource with Multiple Content Types, Media Types, and Carrier Types

Format	Content Type (MARC field 336)	Media Type (MARC field 337)	Carrier Type (MARC field 338)
Book with an accompanying audio CD	text, performed music	unmediated, audio	volume, audio disc
	RDA in MARC		
	336 _ _ $3 book $a text $b txt $2 rdacontent 336 _ _ $3 CD $a performed music $b prm $2 rdacontent 337 _ _ $3 book $a unmediated $b n $2 rdamedia 337 _ _ $3 CD $a audio $b s $2 rdamedia 338 _ _ $3 book $a volume $b nc $2 rdacarrier 338 _ _ $3 CD $a audio disc $b sd $2 rdacarrier		

With RDA, content type, media type, and carrier type are repeatable elements. A bibliographic record for a book with an accompanying audio CD can thus include two types of content, media, and carrier to reflect the two components. Figure 2.10 shows the content types, media types, and carrier types of such a multitype resource. In this example, the MARC encoding includes both subfield $a terms and subfield $b codes. The optional subfield $3 distinguishes which fields belong to which parts of the resource—the book or the CD. Finally, subfield $2 specifies that the terms and codes come from the RDA vocabulary for content, media, and carrier.

Highlight 10: RDA for Content but not Display

The chapters of RDA focus on content, providing catalogers with instructions on recording attributes and relationships—kernels of data that combine to form bibliographic descriptions. RDA does not dictate how these kernels of data are presented within a record or displayed within an online catalog (RDA 0.1). For instance, your library may choose to display bibliographic data using ISBD punctuation (and many likely will), but RDA does not require this. By separating content from display, RDA recognizes that we no longer live in a catalog-card world and opens up current and future possibilities for digital display of bibliographic data.

How to Create an RDA Bibliographic Record

The previous 10 highlights outlined basic RDA concepts and compared them to AACR2. This section applies that knowledge, using a step-by-step approach to catalog a simple printed book. The process begins by answering a series of questions about what you are cataloging. Is the resource a single unit, a serial, or an integrating resource? Is its content communicated via text and perceived through sight or in some other manner? Does accessing its content require any additional device beyond the resource itself? How is its content carried or stored? Is information about the resource taken from the title page or from some other source? Second, the questions shift to ask what information you see on the resource. These elements are transcribed to match exactly what is on the resource, with the possible exceptions of capitalization and punctuation. Finally, the remaining elements are recorded after consulting the resource. These elements document data about the resource but are not directly transcribed from it.

Figure 2.11
Stages of Cataloging a Simple Book

What are you cataloging?	What do you see?	What do you record?
• Mode of issuance	• Title proper	• Extent
• Content type	• Other title information	• Illustrative content
• Media type	• Statement of responsibility	• Color content
• Carrier type	• Creators	• Dimensions
• Preferred source of information	• Contributors	• Notes
	• Publication statement	• Language of the content
	• Edition statement	
	• Title proper of series	
	• Identifier for manifestation	

Figure 2.11 summarizes each stage for cataloging a resource and lists the applicable RDA elements for each. As each phase in the process of cataloging *The Literacy Cookbook* is covered through this chapter, the RDA elements are shown with MARC coding as well as without MARC coding. They are presented with ISBD punctuation, following the instructions provided in Appendix D of RDA (RDA 1.7.3).

What Are You Cataloging?

Figure 2.12 shows the title page and title page verso of *The Literacy Cookbook*, the rush book that is sitting on your desk. Begin by determining the format of the resource in hand. Is it a single unit, a serial, or an integrating resource? Is it a print resource or is it electronic? These decisions are made instinctively and will determine such things as the mode of issuance; content, media, and carrier type; and preferred source of the resource.

Mode of Issuance

The first step in cataloging any type of resource is determining its mode of issuance. This process involves deciding "whether a resource is issued in one

Figure 2.12
Title Page and Title Page Verso of *The Literacy Cookbook*

Title Page	Title Page Verso

The Literacy Cookbook
 	
A PRACTICAL GUIDE TO EFFECTIVE READING, WRITING, SPEAKING, AND LISTENING INSTRUCTION
 	
Sarah Tantillo
 	
With illustrations by Sandy Gingras
 	
JOSSEY-BASS
A Wiley Imprint
www.josseybass.com
	Copyright © 2013 by John Wiley & Sons, Inc. All rights reserved.
	
	Cover design: Jeff Puda
	Cover images © Getty
	
	Published by Jossey-Bass
	A Wiley Imprint
	One Montgomery Street, Suite 1200, San Francisco, CA 94104-4594—www.josseybass.com
	
	No part of this publication may be reproduced, stored in a retrieval system, or transmitted in any form or by any means, electronic, mechanical, photocopying, recording, scanning, or otherwise, except as permitted under Section 107 or 108 of the 1976 United States Copyright Act, without either the prior written permission of the publisher, or authorization through payment of the appropriate per-copy fee to the Copyright Clearance Center, Inc., 222 Rosewood Drive, Danvers, MA 01923, 978-750-8400, fax 978-646-8600, or on the Web at www.copyright.com. Requests to the publisher for permission should be addressed to the Permissions Department, John Wiley & Sons, Inc., 111 River Street, Hoboken, NJ 07030, 201-748-6011, fax 201-748-6008, or online at www.wiley.com/go/permissions.
	
	Permission is given for individual classroom teachers to reproduce the pages and illustrations for classroom use. Reproduction of these materials for an entire school system is strictly forbidden.
	
	Limit of Liability/Disclaimer of Warranty: While the publisher and author have used their best efforts in preparing this book, they make no representations or warranties with respect to the accuracy or completeness of the contents of this book and specifically disclaim any implied warranties of merchantability or fitness for a particular purpose. No warranty may be created or extended by sales representatives or written sales materials. The advice and strategies contained herein may not be suitable for your situation. You should consult with a professional where appropriate. Neither the publisher nor author shall be liable for any loss of profit or any other commercial damages, including but not limited to special, incidental, consequential, or other damages. Readers should be aware that Internet Web sites offered as citations and/or sources for further information may have changed or disappeared between the time this was written and when it was read.
	
	Jossey-Bass books and products are available through most bookstores. To contact Jossey-Bass directly call our Customer Care Department within the U.S. at 800-956-7739, outside the U.S. at 317-572-3986, or fax 317-572-4002.
	
	Wiley publishes a variety of print and electronic formats and by print-on-demand. Some material included with standard print versions of this book may not be included in e-books or in print-on-demand. If this book refers to media such as a CD or DVD that is not included in the version you purchased, you may download this material at **http://booksupport.wiley.com.** For more information about Wiley products, visit **www.wiley.com.**
	
	Library of Congress Cataloging-in-Publication Data
	Tantillo, Sarah, 1965–
	 A practical guide to effective reading, writing, speaking, and listening instruction / Sarah Tantillo; with illustrations by Sandy Gingras.
	  p. cm.
	Includes bibliographical references and index.
	ISBN 978-1-118-28816-0 (pbk.)
	ISBN 978-1-118-33376-1 (ebk.)
	ISBN 978-1-118-33153-8 (ebk.)
	ISBN 978-1-118-33489-8 (ebk.)
	1. Reading. I. Title.
	LB1050.T33 2012
	418'.4—dc23
	                2012030716
	
	Printed in the United States of America
	FIRST EDITION
	
	PB Printing 10 9 8 7 6 5 4 3 2 1

or more parts, the way it is updated, and its intended termination" (RDA Glossary). Single unit, multipart monograph, serial, and integrating resource are the four modes of issuance defined in RDA (RDA 2.13.1.3). Figure 2.13 provides an example of each type of mode of issuance.

Figure 2.13
Examples of Mode of Issuance

Type of Resource	Mode of Issuance
Single volume book	Single unit
PDF file on the Internet	Single unit
Multivolume dictionary	Multipart monograph
Journal	Serial
Website which is updated regularly	Integrating resource

The Literacy Cookbook is an example of a single unit. It is a single volume monograph as opposed to a monograph that has multiple parts. Unlike a serial, it is not a resource that is issued in successive parts with no determined conclusion. It also is not an integrating resource. Updates will not be integrated over time into *The Literacy Cookbook* (RDA 2.13.1.3). Although mode of issuance is not a core element in RDA, it is required for those using OCLC or other bibliographic utilities. As seen in Figure 2.14, a resource's mode of issuance is recorded in the *bibliographic level* element of the MARC leader (i.e., LDR/07 or *BLvl*). Currently in MARC, the value *m* is used for both single unit and multipart monographs.

Figure 2.14
Mode of Issuance

RDA	RDA in MARC
single unit	LDR/07: m

Content Type, Media Type, and Carrier Type

As discussed in Highlight 9 of this chapter, the elements of content type, media type, and carrier type are included in RDA bibliographic records, regardless of the form of the materials or mode of issuance. This information is recorded in two places in a MARC record, first with codes in the MARC leader and then in MARC fields 336, 337, and 338. Figure 2.9 provides examples of content type, media type, and carrier type for common formats.

Content Type   Content type is a core element (RDA 6.9). It is recorded in the *type of record* element of the MARC leader (i.e., LDR/06 or *type*) and subfield $a of MARC field 336. Subfield $2 of field 336 specifies the controlled vocabulary from which the term derives (Figure 2.15). The content of *The Literacy Cookbook* is communicated via *text*. The term comes from the RDA vocabulary for content type.

Figure 2.15
Content Type

RDA	RDA in MARC
text	LDR/06: a
	336 _ _ $a text $2 rdacontent

Media Type   Although media type is not a core element in RDA, it is commonly found in RDA MARC records and is considered core by LC and others (RDA 3.2). The media type term is recorded in MARC subfield $a of field 337. There is not a corresponding element in the MARC leader for a printed book. Subfield $2 of field 337 specifies the controlled vocabulary from which the term derives (Figure 2.16). Accessing the content of *The Literacy Cookbook* does not require an additional device beyond the resource itself. Its media type therefore is *unmediated*. The term comes from the RDA vocabulary for media type.

Figure 2.16
Media Type

RDA	RDA in MARC
unmediated	337 _ _ $a unmediated $2 rdamedia

Carrier Type   Carrier type is a core element (RDA 3.3) and the term is recorded in MARC subfield $a of field 338. There is not a corresponding element in the MARC leader for a printed book. Subfield $2 of field 338 specifies the controlled vocabulary from which the term derives (Figure 2.17). The carrier type for the example book is volume. The term comes from the RDA vocabulary for carrier type.

Figure 2.17
Carrier Type

RDA	RDA in MARC
volume	338 _ _ $a volume $2 rdacarrier

Preferred Source of Information

The resource's mode of issuance and format determine what sources of information are used for an RDA record. Under most individual elements, RDA gives permission to take information from any source, with the choices given in a priority order. The title proper is taken from the preferred source of information (RDA 2.1.2.2). For printed resources, such as *The Literacy Cookbook*, the first choice for the preferred source of information is the resource's title page. It is the most common preferred source of information for a printed resource. If the resource lacks a title page, information is taken from the following parts of the resource in this prescribed order: cover, caption, masthead, colophon, or another part of the resource where the title is located (RDA 2.2.2.2). If a book lacks a title page and other sources of information necessary to identify it, the information is taken from sources outside of the resource, such as a container not issued as part of the book or a published description of the book. If information is taken from outside the resource, it is enclosed in square brackets and a note as to its source is given (RDA 2.2.4).

What Do You See?

Paging through The Literacy Cookbook, you notice the title, the author's name, and a copyright date. You already determined that the preferred source of information for this book is the title page, and the title page verso and other parts of the book provide additional details. You are now ready to add the transcribed elements to the

Mini-Exercise 2.1

What Are You Cataloging?

Match the Content, Media, and Carrier Types with the Type of Resource by putting the appropriate letter next to the resource. For reference, see Figure 2.9 on page 51.

	Content Type	Media Type	Carrier Type
a	spoken word	computer	online resource
b	text, still image	unmediated	volume
c	two-dimensional moving image	video	videodisc
d	cartographic image	unmediated	volume
e	text	computer	online resource

Type of Resource:

1. _____ DVD

2. _____ Atlas

3. _____ Online PDF

4. _____ Graphic novel

5. _____ Downloadable audiobook

bibliographic record, reproducing exactly what you see on the printed page. In this section of Chapter 2, the description of each transcribed RDA element includes figures with side-by-side comparisons showing the data as displayed for patrons to read and as recorded in MARC format.

Title Proper

With possible exceptions such as capitalization and punctuation, information relating to the title proper is transcribed exactly as it appears on the resource in subfield $a of MARC field 245. It is an RDA core element (RDA 1.3, 2.3.1.4, 2.3.2.2). Local practice will dictate whether the capitalization of the title is transcribed as on the item or follows guidelines found in style manuals such as *The Chicago Manual of Style* (RDA 1.7.1, Appendix A). Access and retrieval of a title are not affected by capitalization or punctuation any more than they are affected by the typeface or size of the font.

The title proper for the example book is given with the first letter in each word capitalized, *The Literacy Cookbook*. As with AACR2, the title can be recorded as *The literacy cookbook*, ignoring the capitalization on the resource. It can also be recorded as it appears on the resource, *The Literacy Cookbook*. The authors of this workbook have chosen to follow *The Chicago Manual of Style* for the capitalization of the title in the example record, which, in this case, is also how it appears on the resource (See Figure 2.18).

Figure 2.18
Title Proper

RDA	RDA in MARC
The Literacy Cookbook	245 14 $a The Literacy Cookbook

Other Title Information

This element is not RDA core but is core for the Library of Congress and the Program for Cooperative Cataloging (RDA 2.3.4). Locally, a library could decide not to display the other title information. Other title information (such as a sub-title) that appears on the same source as the title proper is transcribed following the same basic instruction. Information relating to the other title information on the material in hand is transcribed exactly as it appears on the resource. It is given in subfield $b of MARC field 245. The other title information appearing on the example book is in all capital letters. Following *The Chicago Manual of Style* for capitalization in the sample record, the first and last words and all other major words of the other title information are capitalized (See Figure 2.19).

Figure 2.19
Other Title Information

RDA	RDA in MARC
A Practical Guide to Effective Reading, Writing, Speaking, and Listening Instruction	245 14 $a The Literacy Cookbook : $b A Practical Guide to Effective Reading, Writing, Speaking, and Listening Instruction

Statement of Responsibility Relating to Title Proper

The statement of responsibility relating to title proper is core and is transcribed from the same source as the title proper. It is given in subfield $c of MARC field 245. Everything found on the preferred source of information, even titles and degrees of persons, may be included. As discussed in Highlight 8 of this chapter, RDA allows for the abridgement of the statement of responsibility

(RDA 2.4.1.4). However, the LC-PCC policy statement gives the instruction to include all of those named on the preferred source of information in the statement of responsibility, regardless of their function (LC-PCC PS 2.4.1.4). For the example book, two statements of responsibility are listed on the title page—the author, Sarah Tantillo, and the illustrator, Sandy Gingras. Only the first one is required. The second statement of responsibility is optional (See Figure 2.20).

Figure 2.20
Statement of Responsibility

RDA	RDA in MARC
Sarah Tantillo ; with illustrations by Sandy Gingras	245 14 $a The Literacy Cookbook : $b A Practical Guide to Effective Reading, Writing, Speaking, and Listening Instruction / $c Sarah Tantillo; with illustrations by Sandy Gingras.

Creators

The relationship of the creator(s) to the work is recorded in an authorized access point. In RDA, a creator is defined as "a person, family, or corporate body responsible for the creation of a work" (RDA 19.2). As discussed earlier under Highlight 8, the cataloger has more leeway with RDA about the creation of access points. RDA requires only that the first named creator be recorded, but allows the cataloger to record multiple authors, even when there are more than three (RDA 2.4.1.5). It also allows, in such a situation, for the first named author to be the primary access point rather than using the title, as was the rule in AACR2. Although the statement of responsibility relating to the title proper may record all of those listed on the preferred source of information, in RDA, the cataloger is required to create access points only for those with differing primary responsibility.

Sarah Tantillo is considered to be the creator of our example book, *The Literacy Cookbook* (See Figure 2.21). The LC Name Authority File can assist with determining the authorized form of her name, which includes a birth date, for the authorized access point in MARC field 100. More information on the creation of authorized access points is provided in Chapter 3.

Figure 2.21
Creator

RDA	RDA in MARC
Tantillo, Sarah, 1965-	100 1 _ $a Tantillo, Sarah, $d 1965-

Relationship Designators

Relationship designators are optional and were previously discussed in Highlight 8. For the example record, the relationship designator *author* is chosen from Appendix I (See Figure 2.22). This information is recorded in subfield $e of MARC field 100 for personal names or field 110 for corporate authors.

Figure 2.22
Relationship Designator

RDA	RDA in MARC
author	100 1 _ $a Tantillo, Sarah, $d 1965-, $e author.

Contributors

While creators have a relationship to the work, contributors have a relationship to a particular expression. Therefore, as was seen in Chapter 1, an illustrator whose illustrations may be in one expression of a work, but not in another, is a contributor related to that expression. The same situation can be seen with a translator or an editor. Their roles relate to a particular expression, not the work itself.

Relationship designators for contributors come from RDA Appendix I. The information is recorded in subfield $e of MARC field 700 for personal names or field 710 for corporate names.

For *The Literacy Cookbook*, Sandy Gingras was recorded as a contributor (an illustrator) in the statement of responsibility. The cataloger must decide if the role of the contributor merits the creation of an access point. Under LC practice, the first named illustrator must have an access point if the material is intended for children (LC-PCC PS 20.2.1.3). Another consideration is how extensive the illustrations are in the resource or if the contributor is of importance to the cataloger's community. For the example book, the illustrations are not prominent. An access point for the contributor is not needed.

Publication Statement

Place of publication, name of publisher, and date of publication are the three elements of the publication statement and are all RDA core. The information for elements is transcribed and is taken from the preferred source of information as well as other sources, such as the title page verso.

The first element of the statement is the place of publication. It is transcribed as given on the resource in subfield $a of MARC field 264. The city, as well as the name of the larger jurisdiction (e.g., state, province, country), is included if it is found on the resource. For the example book, *The Literacy Cookbook*, San Francisco, CA, is listed on the verso of the title page.

LC-PCC practice is to "supply a probable place of publication, if possible" (LC-PCC PS 2.8.2.6). If a place of publication cannot be found anywhere and no other options are available, a cataloger can record the phrase *Place of publication not identified* in square brackets (RDA 2.8.2). However, if a probable place of publication can be gathered from a source outside of the resource itself, or if a place of distribution or manufacture is available, that place may be recorded in 264 _1 subfield $a and enclosed in square brackets. To support the user tasks, offering a probable place is better than recording *Place of publication not identified.*

The second element of a publication statement is the name of the publisher, which is transcribed in subfield $b of MARC field 264 in the form in which it appears on the source of information. In *The Literacy Cookbook*, the name of the publisher appears on the same source as the title proper. The publisher is listed as an imprint of a larger publishing house. When the name of the publisher is not found on a resource and a probable name cannot be identified from other sources, the phrase *publisher not identified* is supplied in square brackets (RDA 2.8.4). Then the distributor's name or perhaps manufacturer's name (core-if elements) are transcribed in subfield $b of MARC field 264 _2 (distributor) or 264 _3 (manufacturer).

The final element of the statement is date of publication. It is given in subfield $c of MARC field 264. The example book lacks a publication date and contains only the copyright date of 2013. According to LC-PCC policy statement 2.8.6.6, a date of publication that matches the copyright date can be supplied in 264 _1 subfield $c, in square brackets, if it seems reasonable to assume that the copyright date and publication date are the same (See Figure 2.23). If the publication date and copyright differ, then a second MARC field 264 (second indicator 4, subfield $c) with only the copyright date can be used. The copyright symbol, ©, is added before the date. If no publication or copyright date is found, then a date of distribution or manufacture may be used in the publication statement (MARC field 264 _1 subfield $c), again enclosed in square brackets. To support user tasks, the inclusion of a date is strongly encouraged (RDA 2.8.6).

Figure 2.23
Publication Statement

RDA		RDA in MARC	
Place of Publication:	San Francisco, CA	264 _1	$a San Francisco, CA : $b Jossey-Bass, A Wiley Imprint, $c [2013]
Publisher's Name:	Jossey-Bass, A Wiley Imprint		
Date of Publication:	[2013]		

Edition Statement

As noted under Highlight 5 in this chapter, the edition statement is transcribed exactly as it appears on the resource (RDA 2.5, Appendix D.1.2.3). It is given in MARC field 250. Numbers are spelled out if that is how they appear on the source. Edition is abbreviated to *ed.* only when it is abbreviated on the resource. *The Literacy Cookbook*'s edition statement is found on its title page verso. It appears on the source as *First Edition*, not as *1st ed* (See Figure 2.24).

Figure 2.24
Designation of Edition

RDA	RDA in MARC
First Edition	250 _ _ $a First Edition.

Title Proper of Series

The title proper of a series statement is a transcribed, core RDA element. The numbering of a series or subseries is also core if found on the resource (RDA 2.12). International Standard Serial Numbers (ISSNs) associated with series and subseries are core for LC and PCC (RDA 2.12.8). Other elements such as the statement of responsibility relating to the series are optional. Recording series information is similar in RDA and AACR2.

Figure 2.25
Cover of *The Literacy Cookbook*

A series statement, *Jossey-Bass teacher,* can be seen on the cover of *The Literacy Cookbook* (see Figure 2.25), but it lacks series numbering. This information comes from outside of the preferred source of information. The series statement is transcribed in MARC field 490 as shown on the cover, while the authorized access point for the series is recorded in MARC field 830. In this case, the authorized access point is identical to how the series appears on the resource (See Figure 2.26).

Figure 2.26
Title Proper of Series

RDA	RDA in MARC
Jossey-Bass teacher	490 1_ $a Jossey-Bass teacher 830 _0 $a Jossey-Bass teacher.

Identifier for the Manifestation

This element provides data that identifies the manifestation uniquely. International Standard Book Numbers (ISBNs) are used to identify books (RDA 2.15). ISBNs are recorded without hyphens in MARC field 020. A single book can have multiple ISBNs. It can have 13-digit ISBNs as well as 10-digit ISBNs. It can have ISBNs for different manifestations of a book, in which case qualifiers are used to distinguish the manifestations. The title page verso of *The Literacy Cookbook*

Mini-Exercise 2.2

What Do You See?

Identify which of the following transcribed elements are RDA core, RDA core-if, or neither. For reference, see Quick Guide 2.1.

1. _____Title proper

2. _____Other title information

3. _____Statement of responsibility relating to title proper

4. _____Creator

5. _____Relationship designator

6. _____Contributor

7. _____Copyright date

8. _____Edition statement

9. _____Title proper of series

10. _____Identifier for the manifestation

lists four ISBNs. Only the paperback ISBN is part of the printed book's catalog record. The three eBook ISBNs are not part of the record (See Figure 2.27).

Figure 2.27
Identifier for the Manifestation

RDA	RDA in MARC
9781118288160 (pbk.)	020 _ _ $a 9781118288160 (pbk.)

What Do You Record?

Having considered the information that is transcribed, the cataloger now moves to the information from the resource that is recorded. This information includes some of the elements from the description of the carrier and content in an RDA record.

Extent

Extent is defined as "the number of units and/or subunits making up a resource" (RDA Glossary). This information is recorded rather than transcribed. It is given in subfield $a of MARC field 300. *Pages, volumes, leaves,* and *plates* are terms typically used for printed books. Abbreviations are not used for extent. When a book has unnumbered pages and the number of pages can be easily verified, the number of pages is followed by *unnumbered.* The number of pages is preceded by *approximately* when the number of pages cannot be easily verified (RDA 3.4.5.3). If the resource has more than one sequence of paging, the sequences are listed in the order that they appear in the book. *The Literacy Cookbook* has two sequences of paging, xvi preliminary pages and 238 pages of content (See Figure 2.28).

Figure 2.28
Extent

RDA	RDA in MARC
xvi, 238 pages	300 _ _ $a xvi, 238 pages

Illustrative Content

This element is not core for RDA and is core for LC only when the resource is intended for children (RDA 7.15.1, LC-PCC PS for 7.15). Information about illustrations is recorded in subfield $b of MARC field 300 and does not include any abbreviations. RDA provides the option of listing types of illustrations (e.g., charts, maps). LC's policy is to use only the terms *illustration* or *illustrations* (RDA 7.15.1.3). Color illustrations are recorded as *color illustrations, chiefly color illustrations,* or *illustrations (some color),* depending on the number of illustrations that are in color (RDA 7.17.1.3).

The Literacy Cookbook is not intended for children, and its illustrations are of minor importance. Thus, no information about the illustrative content is recorded.

Dimensions

Dimensions for a printed book are recorded in centimeters, with measurements rounded up to the next whole number. For example, if the height of a book is 27.2 centimeters, it is recorded as 28 cm in MARC field 300, subfield $c. Note that *cm* is considered a metric symbol rather than an abbreviation and thus is not followed by a period (RDA 3.5.1.3). However, if a record uses ISBD punctuation and includes a series statement in MARC field 490, then field 300 does conclude with a period. *The Literacy Cookbook* is 23.4 centimeters high, so the dimensions are recorded as 24 cm. (See Figure 2.29).

Figure 2.29
Dimensions

RDA	RDA in MARC
24 cm	300 _ _ $a xvi, 238 pages ; $c 24 cm.

Note Information: Dissertation or Thesis Information,
Summary, Supplementary Content

Additional information about the resource is recorded in notes. If the source of the title is the cover of the book and not the title page, a note is included to indicate the source (e.g. Cover title). Notes about supplementary content, such as the presence of indexes and bibliographical references, are recorded in MARC fields 500 and 504, as appropriate. Dissertation or thesis information is included in MARC field 502 (RDA 7.9). Summary notes are recorded in MARC field 520 (RDA 7.10).

The Literacy Cookbook includes the statement *Grades K-12* on the cover and the spine. It also has a bibliography and an index (See Figure 2.30).

Figure 2.30
Note and Supplementary Content

RDA		RDA in MARC
Note:	"Grades K-12"—Cover.	500 _ _ $a "Grades K-12"—Cover.
Supplementary content:	Includes bibliographical references (pages 219-228) and index.	504 _ _ $a Includes bibliographical references (pages 219-228) and index.

Language of the Content

Although language of the content is not core in RDA, it is required for those using OCLC or other bibliographic utilities and is a core element for LC. It is recorded in fixed field element *language* (i.e., 008/35-37) using the three-letter codes found in the *MARC Code List for Languages*. If it is considered important, a note about the language of the content is recorded in MARC field 546 (RDA 7.12). *The Literacy Cookbook* is written in English (See Figure 2.31).

Figure 2.31
Language of the Content

RDA	RDA in MARC
English	008/35-37: eng

Subject Headings, Classification, and RDA

As of the writing of this book, most chapters in Sections 4, 7, and 10 of RDA have not yet been published. These sections will cover the FRBR Group 3 entities – the concepts, objects, events, and places that comprise subjects. When preparing RDA bibliographic records, catalogers can incorporate subject headings from thesauri such as Library of Congress Subject Headings (LCSH) and Sears Headings, just as they did with AACR2 bibliographic records. With RDA, catalogers can also continue applying classification schemes such as the Library of Congress Classification (LCC) and Dewey Decimal Classification (DCC).

Pulling It All Together

What are you cataloging? What do you see? What do you record? The previous sections answered these questions

Mini-Exercise 2.3

What Do You Record?

Correct the errors in the following MARC fields, formulating the recorded elements according to RDA instructions using ISBD punctuation.

1. 300 _ _ $a 57 pages : $b illustrations (some col.) ; $c 22 cm

_____

2. 300 _ _ $a xii, 492 p. : $b ill. ; $c 28 cm

_____

3. 300 _ _ $a 1 v. (unpaged) : $b chiefly color illustrations ; $c 25 cm
   490 _ _ $a Long lost book series

_____

4. 504 _ _ $a Includes bibliographical references (pp. 219–223) and index.

_____

for *The Literacy Cookbook*. Figure 2.32 brings all of the elements together into a full RDA record.

Figure 2.32
RDA Record for *The Literacy Cookbook*

RDA Element	Data
Title Proper	The Literacy Cookbook
Other Title Information	A Practical Guide to Effective Reading, Writing, Speaking, and Listening Instruction
Statement of Responsibility	Sarah Tantillo ; with illustrations by Sandy Gingras
Designation of Edition	First Edition
Place of Publication	San Francisco, CA
Publisher's Name	Jossey-Bass, A Wiley Imprint
Publication Date	[2013]
Title Proper of Series	Jossey-Bass teacher
Identifier for the Manifestation	9781118288160 (pbk.)
Mode of Issuance	single unit
Media Type	unmediated
Carrier Type	volume
Extent	xvi, 238 pages
Dimensions	24 cm
Content Type	text
Language of Content	English
Note	"Grades K-12"—Cover
Supplementary Content	Includes bibliographical references (p. 219-228) and index
Creator	Tantillo, Sarah, 1965-
Relationship Designator	author

RDA elements are organized according to FRBR concepts and not according to MARC field order. When encoding RDA data in a MARC format, the order of elements is thus different from that found in the RDA instructions. Figure 2.33 shows an RDA record following the order of the MARC record. Also shown are the common MARC field labels, the corresponding RDA elements, and the relevant RDA instruction numbers.

Figure 2.33
Common RDA Elements for a Simple Book in MARC Field Order

MARC Field	MARC Description	RDA Element	RDA Instruction
LDR/06	Type of record: **a**	Correlates to content type	6.9
LDR/07	Bibliographic level: **m**	Mode of issuance	2.13
LDR/18	Descriptive cataloging form: **i** (ISBD punctuation)	—	—
008/35-37	Language code	Language of the content	7.12
020	ISBN	Identifier for the manifestation	2.15
040	Cataloging source: **$e rda**	—	—
100/110	Main entry - personal name/ corporate name	Creator, Relationship designator	19.2, 18.5, Appendix I.2.1
245	Title statement	Title proper, Other title information, Statement of responsibility relating to the title proper	2.3.2, 2.3.4, 2.4.2
250	Edition statement	Designation of edition	2.5.2
264	Publication, Distribution, Manufacture, and Copyright Notice	Place of publication/ Distribution/ Manufacture, Publisher/ Distributor/ Manufacturer, Date of publication/Distribution/ Manufacture/Copyright	2.8, 2.9, 2.10, 2.11
300	Physical description	Extent, Illustrative content, Dimensions	3.4, 7.15, 3.5
336	Content type: **text**	Content type	6.9
337	Media type: **unmediated**	Media type	3.2
338	Carrier type: **volume**	Carrier type	3.3
490/830	Series title statement	Title proper of series, Numbering within series	2.12.2, 2.12.9
504	Bibliography note	Supplementary content	7.16
505	Contents note	Related work	25.1
546	Language note	Language of the content	7.12
700/710	Added entry - personal/ corporate name	Contributor, relationship designator	20.2, 18.5, Appendix I.3.1

Figure 2.34 displays the bibliographic record for *The Literacy Cookbook* in a MARC format. Note the code *i* in the MARC leader *descriptive cataloging form*, and the acronym *rda* in MARC field 040, subfield $e. Both identify this as an RDA record.

Figure 2.34
RDA MARC Record for *The Literacy Cookbook*

LDR/06 (Type)	a	Elvl		Srce		Audn		Ctrl		Lang	eng
LDR/07 (BLvl)	m	Form		Conf	0	Biog		Mrec		Ctry	cau
		Cont	b	GPub		LitF	0	Indx	1		
LDR/18 (Desc)	i	Ills		Fest	0	DtSt	s	Dates	2013,		

040 _ _	$a ### $b eng $e rda $c ###
020 _ _	$a 9781118288160 (pbk.)
100 1 _	$a Tantillo, Sarah, 1965-, $e author.
245 1 4	$a The Literacy Cookbook : $b A Practical Guide to Effective Reading, Writing, Speaking, and Listening Instruction / $c Sarah Tantillo ; with illustrations by Sandy Gingras.
250 _ _	$a First Edition.
264 _ 1	$a San Francisco, CA : $b Jossey-Bass, A Wiley Imprint, $c [2013]
300 _ _	$a xvi, 238 pages ; $c 24 cm.
336 _ _	$a text $2 rdacontent
337 _ _	$a unmediated $2 rdamedia
338 _ _	$a volume $2 rdacarrier
490 1_	$a Jossey-Bass teacher
504 _ _	$a Includes bibliographical references (pages 219-228) and index.
500 _ _	$a "Grades K-12"—Cover.
830 _0	$a Jossey-Bass teacher.

Beyond the Book

RDA was developed to catalog all types of materials, not just printed books. RDA instructions can be applied to sound recordings, moving images, cartographic materials, online resources, both printed and recorded music, and many other material types. Although it is beyond the scope of this workbook to cover all formats in detail, selected MARC records in a variety of formats are included both in the following section (See Figures 2.35–2.39) and on the accompanying CD.

For those seeking further information, some cataloging organizations have developed guidelines or best practices that will guide the cataloger through the RDA Toolkit to cataloging various resources. The *Program for Cooperative Cataloging (PCC) Provider-Neutral E-Resource MARC Record Guidelines* are available for online resources. *Best Practices for Music Cataloging* have been developed by the RDA Music Implementation Task Force of the Music Library Association for both recorded and written music. The OnLine Audiovisual Catalogers (OLAC) are also developing best practices for DVD and Blu-ray discs, and streaming media for both audio and video formats. In addition, some organizations have made available various sample records that will aid catalogers in their work. The Joint Steering Committee for Development of RDA (JSC) has sample RDA records, *Complete Examples—Bibliographic Records*, presented both in MARC and without it. The PCC SCT RDA Records Task Group collected *RDA Record Examples* for a wide variety of resources from simple books to archival resources. Links to all of these resources can be found under the *RDA in Bibliographic Records* portion of the *Useful Resources* section of this workbook.

Sample MARC Records Following RDA Instructions

Figure 2.35
Sample Record for a Provider-Neutral Record for the Electronic Version of *The Literacy Cookbook*

LDR/06 (Type)	a	Elvl		Srce		Audn		Ctrl		Lang	eng
LDR/07 (BLvl)	m	Form	o	Conf	0	Biog		Mrec		Ctry	cau
		Cont	b	GPub		LitF	0	Indx	1		
LDR/18 (Desc)	i	Ills		Fest	0	DtSt	s	Dates	2013,		

040 _ _	$a ### $b eng $e rda $c ###
020 _ _	$a 9781118333761 (ebk.)
020 _ _	$a 9781118331538 (ebk.)
020 _ _	$z 9781118288160 (pbk.)
100 1 _	$a Tantillo, Sarah, 1965-, $e author.
245 1 4	$a The Literacy Cookbook : $b A Practical Guide to Effective Reading, Writing, Speaking, and Listening Instruction / $c Sarah Tantillo ; with illustrations by Sandy Gingras.
250 _ _	$a First Edition.
264 _ 1	$a San Francisco, CA : $b Jossey-Bass, A Wiley Imprint, $c [2013]
300 _ _	$a 1 online resource (xvi, 238 pages).
336 _ _	$a text $2 rdacontent
337 _ _	$a computer $2 rdamedia
338 _ _	$a online resource $2 rdacarrier
490 1_	$a Jossey-Bass teacher
504 _ _	$a Includes bibliographical references (pages 219-228) and index.
500 _ _	$a "Grades K-12"—Cover.
588 _ _	$a Description based on print version record.
776 0 8	$i Print version: $a Tantillo, Sarah, 1965- $t Literacy cookbook. $b First edition $z 9781118288160 $w (DLC) 2012030716 $w (OCoLC)795164252
830 _0	$a Jossey-Bass teacher.
856 4 0	$3 ebrary $u http://site.ebrary.com/lib/librarytitles/docDetail.action ?docID=10629625

Figure 2.36
Sample Record for a Printed Book with Accompanying CD

LDR/06 (Type)	a	Elvl		Srce		Audn		Ctrl		Lang	eng
LDR/07 (BLvl)	m	Form		Conf	0	Biog		Mrec		Ctry	nyu
		Cont		GPub		LitF	0	Indx	1		
LDR/18 (Desc)	i	Ills	a	Fest	0	DtSt	r	Dates	2013,	1985	

006 _ _	innnnb f n
007 _ _	$a s $b d $d u $e u $f n $g g $h n $i n $m e $n u
040 _ _	$a ### $b eng $e rda $c ###
020 _ _	$a 9781442466388
100 1 _	$a Buckley, Richard, $d 1938-, $e author.
245 1 4	$a The foolish tortoise / $c written by Richard Buckley; [illustrated by] Eric Carle.
250 _ _	$a First Little Simon book and CD edition.
264 _ 1	$a New York : b Little Simon, c 2013.
300 _ _	$a 1 volume (unpaged) : $b chiefly color illustrations ; $c 29 cm + $e 1 CD (digital ; 4 3/4 in.)
336 _ _	$3 book $a text $2 rdacontent
336 _ _	$3 CD $a spoken word $2 rdacontent
337 _ _	$3 book $a unmediated $2 rdamedia
337 _ _	$3 CD $a audio $2 rdamedia
338 _ _	$3 book $a volume $2 rdacarrier
338 _ _	$3 CD $a audio disc $2 rdacarrier
347 _ _	$3 CD $a audio file $b CD audio $2 rda
500 _ _	$a Companion CD read by Keith Nobbs.
546 _ _	$a Originally published: [Natick, MA] : Picture Book Studio, 1985.
500 _ _	$a "First edition"—Colophon.
520 _ _	$a "The foolish tortoise wants to move faster, so he decides to leave his heavy shell behind. But then he's too scared to walk anywhere! After some scary encounters, he retraces his steps, climbs back into his home, and bids the world a cheerful 'Good night'. Read along with the enclosed compact disc that contains a charming narration of this classic story!"—Page 4 of cover.
521 _ _	$a Ages 3-7.
700 1 _	$a Carle, Eric, $e illustrator.

Figure 2.37
Sample Record for a DVD

LDR/06 (Type)	g	Elvl		Srce		Audn		Ctrl		Lang	eng
LDR/07 (BLvl)	m	Form		GPub		Time	133	Mrec		Ctry	oru
LDR/18 (Desc)	i	TMat	v	Tech	1	DtSt	s	Dates	2013,		

007 _ _	$a v $b d $d c $e v $f a $g i $h z
040 _ _	$a ### $b eng $e rda $c ###
024 1 _	$a 737885590127
041 0	$a eng $h eng
046 _ _	$k 20121215
245 0 4	$a The Christmas Revels : $b an Appalachian Christmas celebration / $c Portland Revels presents.
257 _ _	$a Portland (Or.) $2 naf
264 _ 1	$a [Portland, Oregon] : $b Portland Revels, $c [2013]
300 _ _	$a 1 videodisc (approximately 133 min.) : $b DVD video, sound, color ; 4 3/4 in.
336 _ _	$a two-dimensional moving image $b tdi $2 rdacontent
337 _ _	$a video $b v $2 rdamedia
338 _ _	$a videodisc $b vd $2 rdacarrier
347 _ _	$a video file $b DVD video $e region all $2 rda
538 _ _	$a DVD-R.
538 _ _	$a This disc is a DVD Recordable and may not play on all DVD equipment.
546 _ _	$a In English.
511 1 _	$a Suzannah Park, Ithica Tell, Nathan Dunkin, Japser Howard, Shuhe Hawkins, Jai Lavette, Hal Day, Illiana Schuring, Jon Kruse, Barbara Millikan, Quinland Porter, Kylie Stanion.
511 0 _	$a Music performed by Portland Brass Quintet.
508 _ _	$a Stage director, Bruce A. Hostetler ; children's director, Hillarie McKenna ; music director, Robert M. Lockwood ; scenic design & set painting, Lawrence Larsen ; script, Gray Eubank, Robert M. Lockwood ; videographer & editor, Christian Bergmans ; producer, DeBorah D. Garman.
518 _ _	$o Recorded $d December 15, 2012 $p Scottish Rite Center, Portland, Oregon.
520 _ _	$a "In 1907 immigration from Europe to the new world of the United States was at a peak. The Irish formed a significant part of this relocation, bringing with them their unique culture of poetry, dance and music plus a powerful instinct for survival"—Revels.org.

500 _ _	$a "18th annual Christmas Revels in Portland."
700 1 _	$a Hostetler, Bruce A., $e stage director.
700 1 _	$a Lockwood, Robert $q (Robert M.), $e musical director, $e screenwriter.
700 1 _	$a McKenna, Hillarie, $e director.
700 1 _	$a Larsen, Lawrence $c (Production designer), $e production designer.
700 1 _	$a Bergmans, Christian, $e director of photography, $e editor of moving image work.
700 1 _	$a Garman, DeBorah D., $e producer.
700 1 _	$a Park, Suzannah, $e actor. *[NOTE: Not all access points are listed in this sample record]*
710 2 _	$a Portland Brass Quintet, $e instrumentalist.
710 2 _	$a Portland Revels, $e presenter, $e publisher.

Figure 2.38
Sample Record for a Magazine

LDR/06 (Type)	a	Elvl		Srce		GPub		Ctrl		Lang	zxx
LDR/07 (BLvl)	s	Form		Conf	0	Freq	b	Mrec		Ctry	nyu
S/L	0	Orig		EntW		Regl	r	Alph	a		
LDR/18 (Desc)	i	SrTp	p	Cont		DtSt	c	Dates	2013,	9999	

040 _ _	$a ### $b eng $e rda $c ###
022 0 _	$a 2327-5014 $2 1
245 0 0	$a Our Wisconsin.
264 _ 1	$a Presque Isle, WI : $b Reiman Wisconsin, LLC
310 _ _	$a Bimonthly
336 _ _	$a text $b txt $2 rdacontent
337 _ _	$a unmediated $b n $2 rdamedia
338 _ _	$a volume $b nc $2 rdacarrier
362 1_	$a Began with Vol. 1, No. 1 (December/January 2013).
500 _ _	$a "... written by neighbors who share your love of Wisconsin"—Cover.
588 _ _	$a Description based on: Vol. 1, No. 1 (December/January 2013); title from cover.
588 _ _	$a Latest issue consulted: Vol. 1, No. 1 (December/January 2013).

Figure 2.39
Sample Record for a Music CD

LDR/06 (Type)	j	Elvl		Srce		Audn		Ctrl		Lang	eng
LDR/07 (BLvl)	m	Form		Comp	uu	AccM		Mrec		Ctry	oru
		Part	n	TrAr	n						
LDR/18 (Desc)	i	FMus	n	LTxt		DtSt	t	Dates	2013,	2013	

007 _ _	$a s $b d $d f $e s $f n $g g $h n $i n $j m $k m $l n $m e
040 _ _	$a ### $b eng $e rda $c ###
100 1 _	$a Suesse, Dana, $d 1909-1987, $e composer.
240 1 0	$a Works. $k Selections
245 1 4	$a Dana Suesse : $b the girl Gershwin / $c Tony Caramia, piano.
264 1 _	$a [Rochester, New York] : $b Eastman School of Music, $c [2013]
300 _ _	$a 1 audio disc : $b CD audio ; $c 4 3/4 in.
336 _ _	$a performed music $2 rdacontent
337 _ _	$a audio $2 rdamedia
338 _ _	$a audio disc $2 rdacarrier
344 _ _	$a digital $b optical $g stereo $2 rda
347 _ _	$a audio file $b CD audio $2 rda
490 1 _	$a Program / Eastman School of Music, University of Rochester ; $v 2012-13
500 _ _	$a Title from disc label.
511 0 _	$a Tony Caramia, piano.
518 _ _	$o Recorded $p Hatch Recital Hall $d 2013 March 26.
500 _ _	$a The 4th event of the 2013 Women in Music Festival.
505 0 0	$t Jazz nocturne $g (1931) (4:12) — $t Rockette $g (1937) (3:06) — $t Afternoon of a black faun $g (1938) (5:06) — $t American nocturne $g (1949, arranged 2011) (4:16) — $t 110th St. rhumba $g (1941) (2:37) — $t Serenade to a skyscraper $g (1941) (5:04) — $t From The cocktail suite: Champagne $g (1942) (3:32) — $t Medley of songs. You oughta be in pictures; My silent love; Have you forgotten; Ho hum $g (8:54) — $t Berceuse $g (2:31) / $r Dana Suesse.
700 1 _	$a Caramia, Tony, e instrumentalist.
700 1 2	$i Contains (work): $a Suesse, Dana, d 1909-1987. $t Jazz nocturne.
700 1 2	$i Contains (work): $a Suesse, Dana, d 1909-1987. $t Rockette.
700 1 2	$i Contains (work): $a Suesse, Dana, d 1909-1987. $t Afternoon of a black faun.
700 1 2	$i Contains (work): $a Suesse, Dana, d 1909-1987. $t American nocturne.
700 1 2	$i Contains (work): $a Suesse, Dana, d 1909-1987. $t 110th Street rumba.

700 1 2	$i Contains (work): $a Suesse, Dana, d 1909-1987. $t Serenade to a skyscraper.
700 1 2	$i Contains (work): $a Suesse, Dana, d 1909-1987. $t Cocktail suite, $p Champagne.
700 1 2	$i Contains (work): $a Suesse, Dana, d 1909-1987. $t Songs. $k Selections.
700 1 2	$i Contains (work): $a Suesse, Dana, d 1909-1987. $t Berceuse, $m piano.
810 2 _	$a Eastman School of Music. $t Program ; $v 2012-13.

Exercise 2.1

Cataloging with RDA

You have five books on your desk that need original cataloging: a lavishly illustrated coffee table book, a guide for parents on early childhood development, an autobiography of a basketball star, a children's book from a popular series on Norse gods, and a picture book. This exercise provides the title page, the title page verso, and some additional information for each of the five books. Complete the following steps to create the bibliographic records.

Step 1 - What are you cataloging? (Worksheet A)

Determine the mode of issuance; content, media, and carrier types; and preferred source of information.

Step 2 - What do you see? (Worksheet B)

Provide data for the transcribed elements such as the title proper and the place of publication. Your library has decided to transcribe information exactly as it appears on the piece.

Hint: Authorized access points for creators and contributors begin with the surname of the person (e.g. Abbe, Miranda K.). For this exercise, do not include dates with the access points. The addition of dates to names will be covered in more detail in Chapter 3 of this workbook.

Step 3 - What do you record? (Worksheet C)

Provide data for the recorded elements such as the extent and dimensions of the book.

Step 4 - RDA in MARC (Worksheet D)

Provide the data in a machine-readable format, in this case MARC. Using ISBD punctuation, transfer the RDA data into the corresponding MARC fields. Worksheet D supplies the MARC indicators and any elements not discussed in Chapter 2.

Note: The worksheet templates are modeled after OCLC's MARC records. Not all elements will be needed for each book.

Book 1	
Title Page	**Title Page Verso**
Nora Peterson **Building Castles and Other Magical Spaces** the architecture of a wizarding world photo-illustrations by Miranda K. Abbe Melbourne 2013 PANDA PRESS	Copyright Nora Elizabeth Peterson. Images copyright M.K. Abbe. PANDA PRESS 100 Collins St Melbourne, Victoria 3001 Also available as an e-book ISBN 9780104112001 ISBN 9780120010411 (ebk)
Additional Information	The book has 250 numbered pages and color photographs on many pages. The height of the book is 30 cm. The book includes a bibliography on pages 240 to 245 and an index.

Book 1: Worksheet A—What Are You Cataloging?

Element	MARC	RDA	Data
Mode of Issuance	LDR/07	2.13.1.3	
Content Type	LDR/06, 336 $a	6.9	
Media Type	337 $a	3.2	
Carrier Type	338 $a	3.3	
Preferred Source of Information	*Not applicable*	2.2.2.2	

Book 1: Worksheet B—What Do You See?

Element	MARC	RDA	Data
Title Proper	245 $a	2.3.2	
Other Title Information	245 $b	2.3.4	
Statement of Responsibility Relating to Title Proper	245 $c	2.4.2	
Creator	100 $a	19.2	
Relationship Designator	100 $e	18.5	
Contributor	700 $a	20.2	
Relationship Designator	700 $e	18.5	
Place of Publication	264 $a	2.8.2	
Publisher's Name	264 $b	2.8.4	
Date of Publication	264 $c	2.8.6	
Copyright Date	264 $c	2.11	
Designation of Edition	250 $a	2.5.2	
Title Proper of Series	490/830 $a	2.12.2	
Numbering within Series	490/830 $v	2.12.9	
Identifier for the Manifestation	020 $a	2.15	

Book 1: Worksheet C—What Do You Record?

Element	MARC	RDA	Data
Extent	300 $a	3.4	
Illustrative Content	300 $b	7.15, 7.17	
Dimensions	300 $c	3.5	
Note	500, 504	2.20, 7.16	
Language of the Content	008/35-37	7.12	

From *The RDA Workbook: Learning the Basics of Resource Description and Access.*
Margaret Mering, Editor. Santa Barbara, CA: Libraries Unlimited. Copyright © 2014

Book 1: Worksheet D—RDA in MARC

LDR/06 (Type)	__	Elvl	Srce	Audn	Ctrl	**Lang**	__
LDR/07 (BLvl)	__	Form	Conf 0	Biog	Mrec	Ctry	at
		Cont b		GPub	LitF 0	Indx	1

LDR/18 (Desc)	__	Ills a	Fest 0	DtSt s	Dates 2013,

040 _ _ $a ### $b eng $e _____ $c ###

020 _ _

100 1 _

245 1 0

264 _ 1

300 _ _

336 _ _

337 _ _

338 _ _

504 _ _

700 1 _

Book 2: Worksheet A—What Are You Cataloging?

Element	MARC	RDA	Data
Mode of Issuance	LDR/07	2.13.1.3	
Content Type	LDR/06, 336 $a	6.9	
Media Type	337 $a	3.2	
Carrier Type	338 $a	3.3	
Preferred Source of Information	*Not applicable*	2.2.2.2	

Book 2: Worksheet B—What Do You See?

Element	MARC	RDA	Data
Title Proper	245 $a	2.3.2	
Other Title Information	245 $b	2.3.4	
Statement of Responsibility Relating to Title Proper	245 $c	2.4.2	
Creator	100 $a	19.2	
Relationship Designator	100 $e	18.5	
Contributor	700 $a	20.2	
Relationship Designator	700 $e	18.5	
Place of Publication	264 $a	2.8.2	
Publisher's Name	264 $b	2.8.4	
Date of Publication	264 $c	2.8.6	
Copyright Date	264 $c	2.11	
Designation of Edition	250 $a	2.5.2	
Title Proper of Series	490/830 $a	2.12.2	
Numbering within Series	490/830 $v	2.12.9	
Identifier for the Manifestation	020 $a	2.15	

Book 2: Worksheet C—What Do You Record?

Element	MARC	RDA	Data
Extent	300 $a	3.4	
Illustrative Content	300 $b	7.15, 7.17	
Dimensions	300 $c	3.5	
Note	500, 504	2.20, 7.16	
Language of the Content	008/35-37	7.12	

Book 2: Worksheet D—RDA in MARC

LDR/06 (Type)	__	Elvl	Srce	Audn	Ctrl	Lang	__
LDR/07 (BLvl)	__	Form	Conf 0	Biog	Mrec	Ctry	nbu
		Cont	GPub	LitF 0	Indx 1		
LDR/18 (Desc)	__	Ills a	Fest 0	DtSt s	Dates 2013,		

040 _ _ $a ### $b eng $e ____ $c ###

020 _ _

100 1 _

245 1 0

250 _ _

264 _ 1

300 _ _

336 _ _

337 _ _

338 _ _

500 _ _

	Book 3	
Title Page		**Title Page Verso**

<table>
<tr>
<td>

DOUBLE

DRIBBLE

MY LIFE IN BASKETBALL

Erik Bowman
and
Ben Bornkamp

©2014

</td>
<td>

©2014 Erik Bowman. All Rights Reserved
Published by Amazing ALLSTARS

First ALLSTAR edition

9780204232010 (hardcover)
9780220100423 (paperback)
9782010042302 (ebook)

</td>
</tr>
</table>

Additional Information	The book has 160 numbered pages. There is a combination of color and black and white photos. The height of the book is 22 cm.

Book 3: Worksheet A—What Are You Cataloging?

Element	MARC	RDA	Data
Mode of Issuance	LDR/07	2.13.1.3	
Content Type	LDR/06, 336 $a	6.9	
Media Type	337 $a	3.2	
Carrier Type	338 $a	3.3	
Preferred Source of Information	*Not applicable*	2.2.2.2	

Book 3: Worksheet B—What Do You See?

Element	MARC	RDA	Data
Title Proper	245 $a	2.3.2	
Other Title Information	245 $b	2.3.4	
Statement of Responsibility Relating to Title Proper	245 $c	2.4.2	
Creator	100 $a	19.2	
Relationship Designator	100 $e	18.5	
Contributor	700 $a	20.2	
Relationship Designator	700 $e	18.5	
Place of Publication	264 $a	2.8.2	
Publisher's Name	264 $b	2.8.4	
Date of Publication	264 $c	2.8.6	
Copyright Date	264 $c	2.11	
Designation of Edition	250 $a	2.5.2	
Title Proper of Series	490/830 $a	2.12.2	
Numbering within Series	490/830 $v	2.12.9	
Identifier for the Manifestation	020 $a	2.15	

Book 3: Worksheet C—What Do You Record?

Element	MARC	RDA	Data
Extent	300 $a	3.4	
Illustrative Content	300 $b	7.15, 7.17	
Dimensions	300 $c	3.5	
Note	500, 504	2.20, 7.16	
Language of the Content	008/35-37	7.12	

From *The RDA Workbook: Learning the Basics of Resource Description and Access.*
Margaret Mering, Editor. Santa Barbara, CA: Libraries Unlimited. Copyright © 2014

Book 3: Worksheet D—RDA in MARC

LDR/06 (Type)	—	Elvl		Srce		Audn		Ctrl		**Lang**	__
LDR/07 (BLvl)	__	Form		Conf	0	Biog		Mrec		Ctry	xx
		Cont		GPub		LitF	0	Indx	0		
LDR/18 (Desc)	__	Ills	a	Fest	0	DtSt	s	Dates	2014,		

040 _ _	$a ### $b eng **$e** _____ $c ###
020 _ _	
020 _ _	
100 1 _	
245 1 0	
250 _ _	
264 _ 1	
300 _ _	
336 _ _	
337 _ _	
338 _ _	
700 1 _	

From *The RDA Workbook: Learning the Basics of Resource Description and Access.*
Margaret Mering, Editor. Santa Barbara, CA: Libraries Unlimited. Copyright © 2014

<table>
<tr><td colspan="2" align="center">**Book 4**</td></tr>
<tr><td align="center">**Title Page**</td><td align="center">**Title Page Verso**</td></tr>
<tr><td>

BRIDGE TO VALHALLA
Book three

DAUGHTERS OF THOR

D. Dillon Halas

mythbooks
Athens Rome Oslo

</td><td>

mythbooks edition published 2013

9780203062004

</td></tr>
<tr><td align="center">**Additional Information**</td><td>The book has 233 numbered pages. The height of the book is 22 cm. There is not an authorized form for the series.</td></tr>
</table>

Book 4: Worksheet A—What Are You Cataloging?

Element	MARC	RDA	Data
Mode of Issuance	LDR/07	2.13.1.3	
Content Type	LDR/06, 336 $a	6.9	
Media Type	337 $a	3.2	
Carrier Type	338 $a	3.3	
Preferred Source of Information	*Not applicable*	2.2.2.2	

From *The RDA Workbook: Learning the Basics of Resource Description and Access.*
Margaret Mering, Editor. Santa Barbara, CA: Libraries Unlimited. Copyright © 2014

Book 4: Worksheet B—What Do You See?

Element	MARC	RDA	Data
Title Proper	245 $a	2.3.2	
Other Title Information	245 $b	2.3.4	
Statement of Responsibility Relating to Title Proper	245 $c	2.4.2	
Creator	100 $a	19.2	
Relationship Designator	100 $e	18.5	
Contributor	700 $a	20.2	
Relationship Designator	700 $e	18.5	
Place of Publication	264 $a	2.8.2	
Publisher's Name	264 $b	2.8.4	
Date of Publication	264 $c	2.8.6	
Copyright Date	264 $c	2.11	
Designation of Edition	250 $a	2.5.2	
Title Proper of Series	490/830 $a	2.12.2	
Numbering within Series	490/830 $v	2.12.9	
Identifier for the Manifestation	020 $a	2.15	

Book 4: Worksheet C—What Do You Record?

Element	MARC	RDA	Data
Extent	300 $a	3.4	
Illustrative Content	300 $b	7.15, 7.17	
Dimensions	300 $c	3.5	
Note	500, 504	2.20, 7.16	
Language of the Content	008/35-37	7.12	

Book 4: Worksheet D—RDA in MARC

LDR/06 (Type)	__	Elvl		Srce		Audn		Ctrl		**Lang**	__
LDR/07 (BLvl)	__	Form		Conf	0	Biog		Mrec		Ctry	it
		Cont		GPub		LitF	0	Indx	0		
LDR/18 (Desc)	__	Ills		Fest	0	DtSt	s	Dates	2013,		

```
040 _ _        $a ### $b eng $e _____ $c ###
020 _ _
100 1 _
245 1 0
250 _ _
264 _ 1
300 _ _
336 _ _
337 _ _
338 _ _
490 0 _
```

Book 5		
Title Page		**Title Page Verso**

Title Page

Easter Egg Hunt

Written by Mikela Kralman
Pictures by Beatrice Kiffmeyer

Title Page Verso

Gretna, Nebraska 2013

ISBN 9780120060630

Additional Information	There are approximately 30 unnumbered pages with color illustrations covering the pages. The height of the book is 20 cm.

Book 5: Worksheet A—What Are You Cataloging?

Element	MARC	RDA	Data
Mode of Issuance	LDR/07	2.13.1.3	
Content Type	LDR/06, 336 $a	6.9	
Media Type	337 $a	3.2	
Carrier Type	338 $a	3.3	
Preferred Source of Information	*Not applicable*	2.2.2.2	

Book 5: Worksheet B—What Do You See?

Element	MARC	RDA	Data
Title Proper	245 $a	2.3.2	
Other Title Information	245 $b	2.3.4	
Statement of Responsibility Relating to Title Proper	245 $c	2.4.2	
Creator	100 $a	19.2	
Relationship Designator	100 $e	18.5	
Contributor	700 $a	20.2	
Relationship Designator	700 $e	18.5	
Place of Publication	264 $a	2.8.2	
Publisher's Name	264 $b	2.8.4	
Date of Publication	264 $c	2.8.6	
Copyright Date	264 $c	2.11	
Designation of Edition	250 $a	2.5.2	
Title Proper of Series	490/830 $a	2.12.2	
Numbering within Series	490/830 $v	2.12.9	
Identifier for the Manifestation	020 $a	2.15	

Book 5: Worksheet C—What Do You Record?

Element	MARC	RDA	Data
Extent	300 $a	3.4	
Illustrative Content	300 $b	7.15, 7.17	
Dimensions	300 $c	3.5	
Note	500, 504	2.20, 7.16	
Language of the Content	008/35-37	7.12	

From *The RDA Workbook: Learning the Basics of Resource Description and Access.*
Margaret Mering, Editor. Santa Barbara, CA: Libraries Unlimited. Copyright © 2014

Book 5: Worksheet D—RDA in MARC

LDR/06 (Type)	__	Elvl		Srce		Audn		Ctrl		**Lang**	__
LDR/07 (BLvl)	__	Form		Conf	0	Biog		Mrec		Ctry	nbu
		Cont		GPub		LitF	0	Indx	0		
LDR/18 (Desc)	__	Ills	a	Fest	0	DtSt	s	Dates	2013,		

040 _ _	$a ### $b eng **$e** ____ $c ###
020 _ _	
100 1 _	
245 1 0	
264 _ 1	
300 _ _	
336 _ _	
337 _ _	
338 _ _	
700 1 _	

From *The RDA Workbook: Learning the Basics of Resource Description and Access.*
Margaret Mering, Editor. Santa Barbara, CA: Libraries Unlimited. Copyright © 2014

Quick Guide to RDA Elements in Bibliographic Records

*Selected RDA elements, their core status, related Group 1 entity,
RDA instruction number, and correlated MARC fields*

What Are You Cataloging?

Element (T=transcribed)	Core	WEMI	RDA	Notes	MARC
Preferred Source of Information	n/a	m	2.2.2.2	*Not an element*	—
Mode of Issuance	LC/PCC Core	m	2.13	Required for those using OCLC or other bibliographic utilities	LDR/07
Media Type	LC/PCC Core	m	3.2	—	337
Carrier Type	RDA Core	m	3.3	—	338
Content Type	RDA Core	e	6.9	—	LDR/06, 336

What Do You See?

Element (T=transcribed)	Core	WEMI	RDA	Notes	MARC
Title Proper (T)	RDA Core	m	2.3.2	Transcribe from preferred source of information	245 $a
Parallel Title Proper (T)	LC/PCC Core	m	2.3.3	—	245 $b
Other Title Information (T)	LC Core	m	2.3.4	—	245 $b
Variant Title (T)	Not Core	m	2.3.6	—	246 $a
Statement of Responsibility Relating to Title Proper (T)	RDA Core	m	2.4.2	If more than one, only the first is required	245 $c
Designation of Edition (T)	RDA Core	m	2.5.2	Statement of responsibility is optional	250 $a

From *The RDA Workbook: Learning the Basics of Resource Description and Access*.
Margaret Mering, Editor. Santa Barbara, CA: Libraries Unlimited. Copyright © 2014

Element (T=transcribed)	Core	WEMI	RDA	Notes	MARC
Date of Production	RDA Core	m	2.7.6	Used for unpublished resources	264 _0 $c
Place of Publication (T)	RDA Core	m	2.8.2	If more than one, only the first is required	264 _1 $a
Publisher's Name (T)	RDA Core	m	2.8.4	If more than one publisher is named, only the first is required	264 _1 $b
Date of Publication	RDA Core	m	2.8.6	Record as found in material	264 _1 $c
Place of Distribution (T)	RDA Core-if	m	2.9.2	If no place of publication, use place of distribution	264 _2 $a
Distributor's Name (T)	RDA Core-if	m	2.9.4	If no publisher's name, use distributor's name	264 _2 $b
Date of Distribution	RDA Core-if	m	2.9.6	If no date of publication, use date of distribution	264 _2 $c
Place of Manufacture (T)	RDA Core-if	m	2.10.2	If no place of publication or distribution, use place of manufacture	264 _3 $a
Manufacturer's Name (T)	RDA Core-if	m	2.10.4	If no publisher or distributor, use manufacturer	264 _3 $b
Date of Manufacture	RDA Core-if	m	2.10.6	If no publication, distribution or copyright date, use date of manufacture	264 _3 $c

What Do You See? (continued)					
Element (T=transcribed)	Core	WEMI	RDA	Notes	MARC
Copyright Date	RDA Core-if	m	2.11	If no publication or distribution date, use copyright date	264 _4 $c
Title Proper of Series (T)	RDA Core	m	2.12.2	LC only uses 490 for series	490/830 $a
ISSN of Series	LC/PCC Core	m	2.12.8	—	490/830 $x
Numbering within Series (T)	RDA Core	m	2.12.9	—	490/830 $v
Identifier for Manifestation (T)	RDA Core	m	2.15	ISBN	020

What Do You Record?					
Element (T=transcribed)	Core	WEMI	RDA	Notes	MARC
Note on Title	LC/PCC Core	m	2.20.2	Source of title, if applicable (e.g., Cover title)	500 $a
Extent	RDA Core-if	m	3.4	Supply only if the resource is complete	300 $a
Dimensions	LC Core	m	3.5	—	300 $c
Intended Audience	LC Core-if	w	7.7	Core element for resources for children	008/22, 521
Dissertation or Thesis Information	LC/PCC Core	w	7.9	—	502 $a
Summarization of the Content	LC Core-if	e	7.10	Core element for children's fiction	520 $a
Language of the Content	LC/PCC Core	e	7.12	—	008/35-37, 041, 546
Illustrative Content	LC Core-if	e	7.15	Core element for Children's resources	300 $b

From *The RDA Workbook: Learning the Basics of Resource Description and Access*.
Margaret Mering, Editor. Santa Barbara, CA: Libraries Unlimited. Copyright © 2014

What Do You Record? (continued)					
Element (T=transcribed)	**Core**	**WEMI**	**RDA**	**Notes**	**MARC**
Supplementary Content	LC Core	e	7.16	For indexes and bibliographies in books	504 $a

Works and Expressions					
Element (T=transcribed)	**Core**	**WEMI**	**RDA**	**Notes**	**MARC**
Preferred Title for Work	RDA Core	w	6.2.2	—	130, 240, 7XX
Form of Work	RDA Core-if	w	6.3	To differentiate	130, 240, 380, 7XX
Date of Work	RDA Core-if	w	6.4	To differentiate	130, 240, 7XX
Place of Origin of the Work	RDA Core-if	w	6.5	To differentiate	130, 240, 7XX
Other Distinguishing Characteristics of the Work	RDA Core-if	w	6.6	To differentiate	130, 240, 7XX
Identifier for Work	RDA Core	w	6.8	Library of Congress Control Number	010
Date of Expression	RDA Core-if	e	6.10	To differentiate	130, 240, 7XX
Language of Expression	RDA Core	e	6.11	—	008/35-37, 041; 546; 130, 240 7XX
Other Distinguishing Characteristics of the Expression	RDA Core-if	e	6.12	To differentiate	130, 240, 7XX
Identifier for Expression	RDA Core	e	6.13	Library of Congress Control Number	010

Relationship to FRBR Group 2 Entities					
Element (T=transcribed)	Core	WEMI	RDA	Notes	MARC
Creator(s)	RDA Core	w	19.2	Only principal responsibility and/or named first required	1XX, 7XX
Others Associated with Work	RDA Core	w	19.3	—	1XX, 7XX
Contributor(s)	LC Core-if	e	20.2	Core element for illustrators of children's resources	7XX
Relationship Designator	n/a	w	18.5, Appendix I.2.1	Creator	1XX, 7XX
		e	18.5, Appendix I.3.1	Contributor	7XX

3

Creating Access Points and Understanding Authority Records

Margaret Mering

The previous chapters discussed the theory behind *Resource Description and Access* (RDA). The first chapter discussed the basic conceptual framework of the *Functional Requirements for Bibliographic Records* (FRBR), including entities, attributes, and relationships. The second chapter studied the basic workflow of cataloging a simple book in RDA. It explored in more detail how to describe the products of intellectual and artistic activities or, in other words, the Group 1 entities of FRBR: works, expressions, manifestations, and items and their attributes. This chapter discusses RDA's guidelines for identifying (i.e., naming) persons, families, corporate bodies, works, and expressions. It will look at the authorized access points of Group 2 entities that are responsible for the intellectual or artistic creation of content, distribution, or ownership of Group 1 entities. It will also consider the authorized access points and preferred titles of works and expressions.

Goals for Chapter 3:
- Introduce elements of authorized access points for persons, families, corporate bodies, works, and expressions.
- Understand how all types of authorized access points are constructed.
- Compare how access points are constructed in RDA and *Anglo-American Cataloguing Rules*, Second Edition (AACR2).
- Learn to read authority records for Group 1 and Group 2 entities.

RDA Chapters 5–6 provide guidelines on identifying and constructing work and expression authorized access points. RDA Chapters 8–11 contain instructions for identifying and constructing person, corporate body, and family access points. These RDA chapters use several key terms. The definitions for these terms are found in the glossary of RDA.

> *Name*: "a word, character, or group of words and/or characters by which a person, family, or corporate body is known."
>
> *Preferred name*: "the form of name chosen as the basis for the authorized access point representing a person, family, or corporate body."
>
> *Variant name*: "a name or form of name by which an entity is known that differs from the name or form of name chosen as the preferred name for that entity."
>
> *Access point*: "a name, term, code, etc. under which information pertaining to a specific entity will be found."
>
> *Authorized access point*: "the standardized access point representing an entity."
>
> *Variant access point*: "an alternative to the authorized access point representing an entity."
>
> *Title*: "a work, character, or group of words and/or characters by which a work is known."
>
> *Preferred title*: "the title or form of title chosen as the basis for the authorized access point representing a work."
>
> *Variant title*: "a title by which a work is known that differs from the title or form of title chosen as the preferred title for that work."
>
> *Creator*: "a person, family, or corporate body responsible for the creation of a work."
>
> *Contributor*: "a person, family, or corporate body contributing to the realization of a work through an expression" (RDA Glossary).

Part 1: Identifying and Constructing Access Points

Persons

RDA Chapter 9 provides instructions for identifying and constructing names of persons. RDA defines a person as "an individual or an identity established by an individual (either alone or in collaboration with one or more other individuals)" (RDA Glossary). Fictitious entities are included as creators and contributors in RDA (RDA 9.0). In previous cataloging codes, fictitious entities were treated as subjects but never as creators and contributors. The fictional comic book mouse Geronimo Stilton can potentially be a creator and a contributor! Figure 3.1 lists the core elements used for personal names.

Figure 3.1
Core Elements for Persons

Core Elements for Persons
Preferred name for person
Date of birth
Date of death
Title of the person
Profession or occupation

Preferred Names for Persons

The preferred name for a person is the most commonly known form. The chosen name can be a person's real name, a nickname, a pseudonym, or some other variation (RDA 9.2.2.3). If a person's name has variant forms, the form found on the first resource received is used as the preferred name. Figure 3.2 provides examples of preferred and variant names of persons.

Figure 3.2
Examples of Preferred and Variant Names

Preferred Name	Variant Name(s)
Sendak, Maurice	—
Carter, Jimmy	Carter, James Earl, Jr.
Eminem	Mathers, Marshall Shady, Slim
Pickford, Mary	Rogers, Mary Pickford Smith, Gladys Mary

If the preferred name includes a surname, words indicating a relationship (e.g., Jr., III) are considered to be part of the commonly known form of a person's name. An example is Martin Luther King, Jr. Terms of address are part of the preferred name when a name consists only of a surname (e.g., Seuss, Dr.) and when a person is identified only by their partner's name (e.g., Barnes, Roy G., Mrs.). A term of address can be included when a name consists only of a first name (e.g., Martha, Cousin; Clara, Miss) (RDA 9.2.2).

If a person writes under more than one name, a preferred name is established for each identity. If an individual writes only under a pseudonym and not under his or her original name, a preferred name is established only for their pseudonym (RDA 9.2.2.8). For example, advice columnist Pauline Phillips wrote only under her pseudonym, Abigail Van Buren. Figure 3.3 provides examples of persons who have written under more than one identity.

Figure 3.3
Examples of Persons Who Write under More than One Identity

Real Name(s)	Pseudonym
Steven King	Richard Bachman
Daniel Handler	Lemony Snicket
Mary O'Shaughnessy, Pamela O'Shaughnessy	Peri O'Shaughnessy

Additions to Preferred Names of Persons

Five possible additions to the preferred name of a person are used to assist in distinguishing persons with the same name. They are added in a prescribed order, as shown in Figure 3.4.

Figure 3.4
Possible Additions to Preferred Name of Persons

Additions	RDA Instruction Number
Title or other designation associated with the person	9.19.1.2
Date of birth and/or death	9.19.1.3
Fuller form of name	9.19.1.4
Period of activity of person	9.19.1.5
Profession or occupation	9.19.1.6

Titles

When applicable, titles of royalty and nobility as well as religious titles are added to the preferred names of persons (RDA 9.19.1.2). Figure 3.5 shows examples of persons' names with titles of royalty and nobility and religious titles.

Figure 3.5
Examples of Persons' Names with Titles of Royalty and Nobility and Religious Titles

Persons' Names with Titles of Royalty and Nobility and Religious Titles
Charles, Prince of Wales, 1948–
Noor, Queen, Consort of Hussein, King of Jordan, 1951–
John Paul II, Pope, 1920–2005

Other Designations Associated with the Person

For Christian saints, *Saint* is part of the preferred name. The word *Spirit* is part of the names of spirits (RDA 9.19.1.2). Figure 3.6 gives examples of Christian saint names and the names of spirits. Essentially, in this context, spirits are ghosts of people.

Figure 3.6
Examples of Christian Saint Names and the Names of Spirits

Christian Saint Names
Cope, Marianne, Saint, 1838–1918
Tekakwitha, Kateri, Saint, 1656–1680
Names of Spirits
Doyle, Arthur Conan, 1859–1930 (Spirit)
Twain, Mark, 1835–1910 (Spirit)

Dates

Birth and death dates distinguish one person from another. *The Library of Congress–Program for Cooperative Cataloging Policy Statement* (LC-PCC PS) for RDA 9.19.1.3 is to apply the option to add dates even if they are not needed to distinguish names. If more than one person has the same name and is born in the same year, the month and the day of birth are included as part of the access point. Complete dates are listed as year-month-date. Months are not abbreviated. Most abbreviations are no longer used with access points. When actual dates are uncertain, *approximate* is used before the date instead of the Latin abbreviation *ca.* (i.e., circa), which was used under AACR2. Hyphens are used instead of *b.* or *d.* for birth and death dates (RDA 9.19.1.3). Figure 3.7 provides examples of persons' names which include dates.

Figure 3.7
Examples of Persons' Names which Include Dates

Persons' Names That Include Dates
Thorp, Frank, Jr. 1900–1955
Johnson, Mark, 1957 August 5–
Johnson, Mark, 1957 June 17–
Johnson, Mark, 1957 November 2–
Foster, John Alexander Hastings, –1876
Barnard, Samuel, approximately 1788–1838
Messalla Corvinus, Marcus Valerius, 64 B.C.–approximately 8 A.D.

Core-if Elements for Persons

The fuller form of name, the period of activity, and the profession or occupation of a person are added to the preferred name only if they are needed to distinguish a person from another person with the same name. They are referred to as *core-if* elements. If neither the birth date nor the death date are known, the period of years in which the person was active in his or her profession or other endeavors may be added to the preferred name. If a fuller form of the name and dates of a person are unknown or if the name does not convey the idea of a person, the person's occupation or profession can be added to the name. Unlike AACR2, a person's occupation or profession is always enclosed in parentheses (RDA 9.19.1.4-9.19.1.6). Figure 3.8 gives examples of persons' names with core-if elements.

Figure 3.8
Examples of Persons' Names with Core-if Elements

Persons' Names with Fuller Form of Name
Smith, Chris (Christopher Anthony) Smith, Chris (Christopher Corey)
Walsh, P.J. (Pat J.) Walsh, P.J. (Peter J.)
Persons' Names with Dates Active in Profession
Aiken, James, active 1878
Beard, Nancy, active 19th century
Bernstein, Melvin, active 1945–1946
Persons' Names with Profession
Crank! (Letterer)
Lacey, Helen (Writer of love stories)
Martin, Jay (Soccer coach)
Freedman, Alan (Museum director)
Miller, Chris (Postcard collector)

Families

RDA Chapter 10 provides instructions for identifying and constructing names of families. RDA defines a family as "two or more persons related by birth, marriage, adoption, civil union, or similar legal status, or who otherwise present themselves as a family" (RDA Glossary). Under RDA, family names can be creators and contributors as well as subjects. Families could only be subjects under AACR2. Considering families as creators and contributors is especially helpful to archives and museums. Figure 3.9 lists the core elements used for family names.

Figure 3.9
Core Elements for Families

Core Elements for Families
Preferred name for family
Type of family
Date of associated with the family

The preferred name is taken from the resource being cataloged. It can also be taken from other formal statements in resources associated with the family and reference sources (RDA 10.2.2). Any source can be used to determine the type of family and dates associated with a family. As of the writing of this

text, there is not a controlled vocabulary for the type of family element. *Family, Royal house*, and *Dynasty* are examples of terms used with this element (RDA 10.3; 10.10.1.2). The dates represent significant dates associated with a family, not the entire history of a family (RDA 10.4; 10.10.1.3).

A place associated with the family and a prominent family member are possible core-if elements that can be added to the preferred name if needed to distinguish one family from another with the same name. The place and the family member's name are both given in the same form as they would be if they were authorized access points (RDA 10.5-10.6; 10.10.1.4-10.10.1.5). Figure 3.10 provides examples of family names with core and core-if elements.

Mini-Exercise 3.1

Persons and Families

Select the correct RDA access points.

1. a. Sandford, John, 1944 Feb. 23–
    b. Sandford, John, 1944 February 23–

2. a. Madonna, 1958–
    b. Ciccone, Madonna Louise Veronica, 1958–

3. a. O'Keefe, James (Automobile racing history)
    b. O'Keefe, James, Automobile racing historian
    c. O'Keefe, James (Automobile racing historian)

4. a. Pasquali, Nicolo, approximately 1718–1757
    b. Pasquali, Nicolo, ca. 1718–1757

5. a. Calder (1757–1959 : N.C.)
    b. Calder (Family : 1757–1959 : N.C.)

Figure 3.10
Examples of Family Names

Family Names
Baroni (Family : Natchez, Miss.)
Agrant (Family : 1894–1976 : S.D.)
Carmen (Family : Carman, Thomas, 1815–1899)
Romanov (Dynasty : 1613–1917)
Chichibu no Miya (Royal House)

Corporate Bodies

RDA Chapter 11 provides instructions for identifying and constructing names of corporate bodies. RDA defines corporate bodies as "an organization or group of persons and/or organizations that is identified by a particular name and that acts, or may act, as a unit" (RDA Glossary). Corporate bodies include associations, corporations, government agencies, projects and programs, names of churches, religious and musical groups, and conferences. Vessels (e.g., ships and spacecraft) and ad hoc events (e.g., athletic contests, exhibitions, festivals) are also considered to be corporate bodies (RDA 11.0).

As with names of persons, the preferred name for a corporate body is the most commonly known form. If a corporate body's name has variant forms, the form found on the first resource received is used as the preferred name. The spelled out form of *Department* is used instead of the abbreviation *Dept.* (RDA 11.2.2).

Place, institution, and date are core-if elements for corporate bodies. A place associated with the corporate body is usually the location of its headquarters. The place is given in the same form as its authorized access point. The institution associated with the corporate body will sometimes better identify it than a place. The institution may be better known or more meaningful than a place. It is given in its preferred form, but not necessarily in its authorized access form (RDA 11.3). The beginning and the ending dates of a corporate body can also be used to break a conflict between two corporate bodies. Dates are often used to distinguish earlier and later names of the same corporate body (RDA 11.4). A word or a phrase qualifier can be used to distinguish the names of corporate bodies. When the name of a corporate body does not convey the idea of a corporate body, a word or a phrase qualifier can also be used (RDA 11.7.1.4). Figure 3.11 shows examples of corporate bodies' names with core-if elements.

Figure 3.11
Examples of Corporate Bodies' Names with Core-if Elements

Corporate Body Names	
With **place** qualifiers	Yellow Ribbon Movement (Philippines) First Baptist Church (Oxford, Ohio)
With **institution** qualifiers	Program for Exceptionally Gifted Children (Mary Baldwin College)
With **date** qualifiers	Paramount Pictures Corporation (1914–1927)
With **phrase** qualifiers	PrairieWorks (Firm) Debs (Musical group) New Orleans (Cruiser) USDA Food Safety Discovery Zone (Mobile classroom)

Conferences, etc.

As noted earlier in this chapter, conferences are a type of corporate body. When applicable, under RDA, frequency is part of the preferred name of a conference. Under AACR2, frequency was not included as part of conference access points (RDA 11.2.2). When cataloging monographs, the place where the conference was held is a core element of a conference name (RDA 11.3).In some instances, the institution associated with a conference is used because it better identifies the conference (RDA 11.5). The date a conference was held is also a core element (RDA 11.4.2). The number of a conference is a core element when applicable. Numbers are recorded as ordinal numbers (i.e., 1st, 2nd) (RDA 11.6). A word or phrase qualifier is used when the conference name does not convey the idea of a conference (RDA 11.17.1.4). Figure 3.12 provides examples of conference access points.

Mini-Exercise 3.2
Corporate Bodies

Select the correct RDA access points.

1. a. Nebraska. Department of Social Services
    b. Nebraska. Dept. of Social Services

2. a. Tenth Advances in Computer Games (2003 : Graz, Austria)
    b. Advances in Computer Games (Conference) (10th : 2003 : Graz, Austria)

3. a. 10 Mile Crossing (Musical group)
    b. 10 Mile Crossing

4. a. St. Mark's Episcopal Church
    b. St. Mark's Episcopal Church (Evanston, Ill.)

Figure 3.12
Examples of Conference Names

Conference Names
JAMI Conference (2011 : Baltimore, Md.)
Annual Conference on Book Trade History (31st : 2009 : Bloomsbury, London, England)
Asian Congress of Fluid Mechanics (13th : 2010 : Islamic University of Technology)
Is U.S. Government Debt Different? (Conference) (2012 : Wharton School)

Works

RDA Chapter 6 provides instructions for *identifying* and *constructing* names of works. As noted in Chapter 1 of this book, RDA and FRBR define work as "a distinct intellectual or artistic creation" (RDA Glossary). The first part of the authorized access point of a work is the authorized form of the creator's name, if applicable. The second part of the access point is the preferred title. Preferred title is "the title or form of title chosen as the basis for the authorized access point representing a work" (RDA Glossary).

If needed, form of work (i.e., genre), date, place of origin, or other distinguishing characteristics of the work can be added to differentiate one work from another work. One or more of these qualifiers can be added to the access point. If there is no conflict, none of these attributes need to be added. This process of establishing the authorized access point for a work was referred to in AACR2 as determining the main entry.

For both RDA and AACR2, as shown by the example in Figure 3.13, the authorized access point for a work created by one person, family, or corporate body includes the creator and the preferred title.

Figure 3.13
Example of Authorized Access Point and Preferred Title

Authorized Access Point	Preferred Title
Twain, Mark, 1835–1910	The Adventures of Tom Sawyer

Unlike AACR2, RDA has no rule of three for creators when constructing an authorized access point for a work. A work with four or more authors is set up as an author/title authorized access point. The author who has principal responsibility for the work and/or is named first is listed as the creator. It does not become a title authorized access point. Under AACR2, the main entry for the Figure 3.14 example is *A Think-Aloud and Talk-Aloud Approach to Building Language*. Under RDA, Reuven Feuerstein is part of the authorized access point.

Figure 3.14
Authorized Access Points for a Work with Four or More Creators

AACR2	
245 02	$a A think-aloud and talk-aloud approach to building language : $b overcoming disability, delay, and deficiency / $c Reuven Feuerstein . . . [et al.] ; foreword by Yvette Jackson.
RDA	
100 1_	$a Feuerstein, Reuven.
245 12	$a A think-aloud and talk-aloud approach to building language : overcoming disability, delay, and deficiency / $c Reuven Feuerstein, Louis H. Falik, Refael S. Feuerstein, & Krisztina Bohács ; foreword by Yvette Jackson.

Source of Preferred Title

For works created after 1500, the preferred title is established by consulting the first edition of the work and reference sources. Under RDA, unlike AACR2, unrevised and revised editions are treated in the same manner. The title of the first edition is listed in MARC field 240 and is considered to be the preferred title, as shown in Figure 3.15 (RDA 6.2.2.2). This type of title was called a uniform title under AACR2. Authority records are created for unrevised and revised editions under RDA.

Figure 3.15
Preferred Title for a Revised Edition under RDA

100 1_	$a Wittenberg, Eric J., $d 1961–
240 10	$a Protecting the flank
245 10	$a Protecting the flank at Gettysburg : $b the battles for Brinkerhoff's Ridge and East Cavalry Field, July 2–3, 1863 / $c Eric J. Wittenberg.
250 _ _	$a First Savas Beatie edition, completely revised and expanded.
264 _1	$a El Dorado Hills, California : $b Savas Beatie LLC, $c 2013.
500 _ _	$a Original title: Protecting the flank.

Compilations of Works

The collective title *Works* is used as the preferred title for the complete compilation of works by a single creator who writes in more than one form. For creators who write in only one particular form, suggested terms *correspondence, essays, novels, plays, prose works, short stories,* and *speeches* are used to create the preferred title. If none of these terms apply, more appropriate terms can be used (e.g., *Fairy tales*). For compilations, which consist of two or more works by a single author, but are not all of their publications, *Works. Selections* is added to the preferred title. Under AACR2, the word *Selections* was used alone for selected publications of writers who wrote in more than one format (RDA 6.2.2.10.3). Figure 3.16 gives examples of collective titles used as preferred titles.

According to RDA instructions, in addition to a collective title, access points are given for the individual works of a

Figure 3.16
RDA Examples of Collective Titles Used as Preferred Titles

RDA Examples of Collective Titles Used as Preferred Titles	
100 1_	$a Twain, Mark, $d 1835-1910.
240 10	$a Works
245 14	$a The complete works of Mark Twain
100 1_	$a Twain, Mark, $d 1835-1910.
240 10	$a Works. $k Selections
245 14	$a The wit and wisdom of Mark Twain
100 1_	$a Twain, Mark $d 1835-1910.
240 10	$a Essays
245 14	$a The complete essays of Mark Twain
100 1_	$a Twain, Mark $d 1835-1910.
240 10	$a Novels. $k Selections
245 14	$a The gilded age and later novels

compilation. Giving an access point for the first work of a compilation is a requirement. Providing access points for the other titles of a compilation is optional. The bibliographic record may also have a contents note listing the individual works (RDA 6.2.2.10.3). Under AACR2, for compilations of only two works by one creator, the title of the first work was given in MARC field 240 as a uniform title. For the Figure 3.17 example, *Novels. Selections* is the preferred title under RDA. *The Adventures of Tom Sawyer* was called the uniform title under AACR2.

Figure 3.17
Collective Titles for Two Works by One Creator

AACR2	
100 1_	$a Twain, Mark, $d 1835-1910.
240 10	$a Adventures of Tom Sawyer
245 10	$a The adventures of Tom Sawyer ; The adventures of Huckleberry Finn / $c Mark Twain.
700 12	$a Twain, Mark $d 1835-1910. $t Adventures of Huckleberry Finn.
RDA	
100 1_	$a Twain, Mark, $d 1835-1910.
240 10	$a Novels. $k Selections.
245 10	$a The adventures of Tom Sawyer ; The adventures of Huckleberry Finn / $c Mark Twain.
700 12	$a Twain, Mark $d 1835-1910. $t Adventures of Tom Sawyer
700 12	$a Twain, Mark $d 1835-1910. $t Adventures of Huckleberry Finn.*
	*optional field

Motion Pictures and Television and Radio Programs

The preferred titles of motion pictures and television and radio programs include forms of the works. These terms are added in parentheses to the preferred title. They are added to help convey the idea of a motion picture, television program, and radio program. They can also distinguish like titles (RDA 6.3). Figure 3.18 gives examples of preferred titles for motion pictures and television and radio programs.

Figure 3.18
Examples of Preferred Titles for Motion Picture and Television and Radio Programs

Preferred Titles for Motion Picture and Television and Radio Programs
Planet of the apes (Motion picture : 1968)
Planet of the apes (Motion picture : 2001)
Planet of the apes (Television program)
This American Life (Radio program)

Parts of the Bible

There are two differences between RDA and AACR2 for the preferred titles of parts of the Bible. RDA uses the spelled out forms of *Old Testament* and *New Testament* instead of *O.T.* and *N.T.* The name of the testament is omitted from the preferred titles of individual books or groups of books (RDA 6.23.2.9). Figure 3.19 provides examples of preferred titles for parts of the Bible.

Figure 3.19
Preferred Titles for Parts of the Bible

AACR2	RDA
Bible. O.T.	Bible. Old Testament
Bible. N.T.	Bible. New Testament
Bible. O.T. Ezra	Bible. Ezra
Bible. N.T. Gospels	Bible. Gospels

Expressions

RDA Chapter 6 provides instructions for identifying and constructing names of expressions. RDA and FRBR define an expression as "the intellectual or artistic realization of a work in the form of alpha-numeric, musical or choreographic notation, sound, image, object, movement, etc., or any combination of such forms" (RDA Glossary). An expression's authorized access point for a resource starts with its work's authorized access. Content type, date, language, or other distinguishing characteristics are added to make the expression's authorized access point unique.

As discussed in Chapter 1 of this workbook, Mark Twain's *The Adventures of Tom Sawyer* has numerous expressions. A Spanish translation is one example of an expression. As shown in Figure 3.20, its authorized access point is *Twain, Mark, 1835-1910. Adventures of Tom Sawyer*. The authorized access point for a Spanish translation of the resource is *Twain, Mark, 1835-1910. Adventures of Tom Sawyer. Spanish.*

Figure 3.20
Authorized Access Point for Spanish Translation

100 1_	$a Twain, Mark, $d 1835-1910.
240 10	$a Adventures of Tom Sawyer. $l Spanish
245 14	$a Las adventuras de Tom Sawyer / $c Mark Twain.

Mini-Exercise 3.3
Works and Expressions

Select the correct RDA access points.

1. a. Bible. N.T. Revelation
    b. Bible. New Testament. Revelation
    c. Bible. Revelation

2. a. Barney Miller (Television program)
    b. Barney Miller

3. a. Lewis, C. S. (Clive Staples), 1898–1963. Selections
    b. Lewis, C. S. (Clive Staples), 1898–1963. Works. Selections

4. a. Lenski, Lois, 1893–1974. Cowboy Small. Spanish & English
    b. Lenski, Lois, 1893–1974. Cowboy Small. Spanish
    c. Lenski, Lois, 1893–1974. Vaquero Pequeño. Spanish & English
    d. Lenski, Lois, 1893–1974. Cowboy Small. English

If the original English language expression and the Spanish translation are published as a compilation, an analytical authorized access point is given for each expression. Under AACR2, the different expressions were given together in subfield $l of uniform title MARC field 240, as shown in Figure 3.21 (RDA 6.11).

Figure 3.21
Compilation of the English and Spanish Language Expressions of the Same Work

AACR2	
100 1_	$a Twain, Mark, $d 1835-1910.
240 10	$a Adventures of Tom Sawyer. $l Spanish & English
245 14	$a The adventures of Tom Sawyer = $b Las adventuras de Tom Sawyer / $c Mark Twain.
246 31	$a Adventuras de Tom Sawyer
546 _ _	$a English and Spanish.
RDA	
100 1_	$a Twain, Mark, $d 1835-1910.
245 14	$a The adventures of Tom Sawyer = $b Las adventuras de Tom Sawyer / $c Mark Twain.
246 31	$a Adventuras de Tom Sawyer
546 _ _	$a English and Spanish.
700 12	$a Twain, Mark, $d 1835-1910. $t Adventures of Tom Sawyer
700 12	$a Twain, Mark, $d 1835-1910. $t Adventures of Tom Sawyer $l Spanish

Part 2: Authority Records

Authority records include information about authorized forms of names, subjects, and titles and are used when establishing authorized access points. Although not all catalogers create authority records for the Name Authority Cooperative Program (NACO), or even locally, understanding the information in an authority record is an important aspect of cataloging. The Library of Congress's authority files are available at http://authorities.loc.gov/. The records are available in MARC form and in non-MARC label form. These authority records can be downloaded to local catalogs free of charge. OCLC also provides access to the Library of Congress's authority files for a fee. This workbook's accompanying CD includes a Quick Guide for Authority Records, which shows tables with the MARC terms, the MARC tags, MARC subfields, and RDA instruction numbers for the elements of persons, families, corporate bodies, works, and expressions.

Persons, Families, and Corporate Bodies

Most elements of authority records for persons, families, and corporate bodies are self-explanatory. Many of the elements have already been described in this chapter. Others help to further confirm that the correct name has been identified and to distinguish entities with the same or similar names. Information provided in authority records can help to differentiate names now as well as in the future. Figure 3.22 is the personal name authority record for singer and actress Cher.

All name authority records, whether they are for a person, a family, or a corporate body, include an authorized access point. Personal names are given in MARC field 100 with a first indicator of 1 or 0 (i.e., 100 1_ or 100 0_) depending on whether a name has both a first and a last name or only a first name. In Figure 3.22, *Cher, 1946-* is the authorized access point. Family names also use MARC field 100 and have a first indicator of 3 (i.e., 100 3_). Corporate names are listed in MARC field 110. Conference names are recorded in MARC field 111.

All name authority records also include MARC fields 010, 040, and 670. The 010 includes the Library of Congress Control Number (LCCN), which serves as the unique identifier of the authorized access point. The LCCN for the authority record for Cher is *n 50038010*. The 040 includes the National Union Catalog (NUC) symbols of the libraries that created or modified the record. For an RDA authority record prepared by an English-language cataloging agency, it also includes subfields $b eng and $e rda. The 670 includes the source on which the access point was based and the information found. This information may also be listed in other MARC fields with elements to which it applies. The authority record in Figure 3.22 includes three 670 MARC fields. They list the sources used to establish Cher's name and variants of her name. The third 670 tells us that she legally changed her name to Cher without a surname in 1979.

Figure 3.22
Personal Name Authority Record for Cher

010 _ _	$a n 50038010
040 _ _	$a ### $b eng $e rda $c ###
046 _ _	$f 19460520
100 0_	$a Cher, $d 1946-
374 _ _	$a Singer $a Actress
375 _ _	$a female
377 _ _	$a eng
400 1_	$a Sarkisian, Cherilyn, $d 1946-
400 1_	$a Bono, Cher, $d 1946-
400 1_	$a Allman, Cher, $d 1946-
400 1_	$a Sakesian, Cherilyn, $d 1946-
400 1_	$a Sakisian, Cherilyn, $d 1946-
400 1_	$a La Piere, Cherilyn, $d 1946-
400 1_	$a LaPierre, Cherilyn, $d 1946-
400 0_	$a Cleo, $d 1946-
510 2_	$w r $i Group member of: $a Sonny & Cher
670 _ _	$a Jacobs, L. Cher, 1975: $b t.p. (Cher)
670 _ _	$a Bronaugh, R.B. Celebrity birthday book, c1981: $b p. 38 (Cher; singer-actress; b. Cherilyn Sarkisian (or Sakisian) (or Cherilyn La Piere) 5/20/1946)
670 _ _	$a Wikipedia, Apr. 18, 2009 $b (Cher, b. Cherilyn Sarkisian on May 20, 1946; also known as: Cherilyn LaPierre; Cleo; Cher Bono; in 1979 legally changed her name to: Cher, no surname)
678 _ _	$a Cher (1946-) is an American singer and actress.

Other elements may optionally be included in all types of name authority records to assist with identifying and differentiating names. For example, authority records for persons, families, and corporate bodies can include variant names. Variant names for persons are listed in MARC field 400, first indicator 1 or 0. Family variant names are listed in MARC field 400, first indicator 3. Corporate body variant names are recorded in MARC fields 410 or 411. The authority record for Cher (Figure 3.22) includes eight different variant names.

Dates

Dates associated with persons, families, and corporate bodies are given in MARC field 046. They are recorded according to International Organization for Standardization standard ISO 8601. Dates are formatted as YYYYMMDD.

According to the Figure 3.22 authority record, Cher's birth date is May 20, 1946. The date is encoded as 046 _ _ $f 19460520.

Places

Places associated with persons, families, and corporate bodies are given in MARC field 370. Cher's authority record (Figure 3.22) does not include a 370. The authority record for Martin Luther King, Jr. gives his places of birth and death. They are listed as 370 _ _ $a Atlanta, Ga. $b Memphis, Tenn. Subfields $a and $b of the 370 are used only for personal names. For all types of names, subfield $c of the 370 is used for countries associated with the person, family, or corporate body. Subfield $e is used for the place a family lives, the location of a conference, or the headquarters of a corporate body. Subfield $f is used for other places associated with a family, a corporate body, or a conference.

The relationships between persons, families, and corporate bodies are given in authority records in MARC fields 500, 510, and 511. RDA Chapters 29–32 cover these types of relationships. Relationship designators that are found in RDA Appendix K are listed in subfield $i of these fields to identify different types of relationships. Subfield $w with code *r* is used to indicate that the MARC field has a relationship designator in subfield $i. For corporate bodies, subfield $w with the codes *a* and *b* can be used to show earlier and later names. Figure 3.23 shows examples of relationships found in authority records.

Figure 3.23
Examples of Relationships in Authority Records

Relationships between Persons, Families, and Corporate Bodies	
100 0_	$a Cher, $d 1946-
510 2_	$w r $i Group member of: $a Sonny & Cher
100 1_	$a Socks $c (Cat), $d 1989-2009
500 1_	$w r $i Owner: $a Clinton, Bill, $d 1946-
500 1_	$w r $i Owner: $a Currie, Betty
100 1_	$a Schickele, Peter
500 1_	$w r $i Alternate identity: $a Bach, P. D. Q., $d 1742-1807
100 3_	$a Baroni (Family : $c Natchez, Miss.)
500 1_	$w r $i Progenitor: $a Baroni, Majorie Rushing, $d 1924-1986
110 1_	$a Jacksonville (Fla.). $b Jacksonville Fire Department
510 1_	$w b $a Jacksonville (Fla.) $b Fire Protection Division
110 2_	$a Karin Newby Gallery & Sculpture Garden
510 2_	$w r $i Predecessor: $a Karin Newby Gallery

Languages

The languages used by persons and corporate bodies are recorded in MARC field 377. The languages identified in the authority record are the ones the person writes in or a corporate body communicates in for their publications, and not necessarily the language of the country where they live or are located. The three-letter language codes from the *MARC Code List for Languages* are used instead of the spelled out forms of the languages. The language listed for Cher's authority record (Figure 3.22) is *eng* (i.e., English).

Field of Activity

Field of activity, another element used in authority records for persons and corporate bodies, consists of topical subject terms that cover areas of endeavor and expertise. Field of activity is recorded in MARC field 372. Field of activity may seem very similar to the profession or occupation element. Terms used for occupation are expressed as classes of persons rather than as topical subject terms. Field of activity is not used as part of access points. Professions or occupations can be used as part of an access point to distinguish like names. They are also given in MARC field 374 of an authority record. Figure 3.24 compares the profession or occupation terms used in Figure 3.8 with field of activity terms.

Figure 3.24
Comparison of Occupations and Fields of Activity

Occupations	Fields of Activity
Letterer	Comic books, strips, etc. Graphic novels
Writer of love stories	Love stories
Soccer coach	Soccer – Coaching
Museum director	Jewish sports history
Postcard collector	Postcards – Collectors and collecting Winona (Minn.) – History Local history

Fuller Form of Name

Fuller form of name and gender are two elements in authority records that are used only for authority records for persons. Fuller form of name is recorded in MARC field 378. It may also, but will not always, be part of the authorized access point. Gender is given in MARC field 375. Knowing a person's gender may help confirm that the correct person has been found, especially when the person's name is in a language that the cataloger is not familiar with or when the person has a gender-neutral name.

Works and Expressions

Figure 3.25 is an example of an authority record for a preferred title of a motion picture. Figure 3.26 is an example of an authority record for a collective title. Figure 3.27 is an example of an authority record for a Spanish translation of an original English-language expression.

Figure 3.25
Example of an Authority Record for a Preferred Title of a Motion Picture

010 _ _	$a no2001058175
040 _ _	$a ### $b eng $e rda $c ###
046 _ _	$k 2001
130 _0	$a Planet of the apes (Motion picture : 2001)
380 _ _	$a Motion picture
500 1_	$w r $i Motion picture adaptation of (work): $a Boulle, Pierre, $d 1912-1994. $t Planète des singes
530 _0	$w r $i Remake of (work): $a Planet of the apes (Motion picture : 1968)
670 _ _	$a Planet of the apes : original motion picture soundtrack, p2001.
670 _ _	$a Wikipedia, January 24, 2011 ‡b (Planet of the Apes is a 2001 American science fiction film...)

Figure 3.26
Example of an Authority Record for a Collective Title

010 _ _	$a n 2013006336
040 _ _	$a ### $b eng $e rda $c ###
100 1_	$a Twain, Mark, $d 1835-1910. $t Works. $k Selections
400 1_	$a Twain, Mark, $d 1835-1910. $t Wit and wisdom of Mark Twain
670 _ _	$a The wit and wisdom of Mark Twain, 2013 ‡b CIP introductory [editor's] note ("The quotations I've gathered here ...")

Figure 3.27
Example of an Authority Record for a Spanish Translation of an Original English-Language Expression

010 _ _	$a n 2012011130
040 _ _	$a ### $b eng $e rda $c ###
100 1_	$a Cusimano, Maryann K. $t You are my I love you. $l Spanish
377 _ _	$a spa
400 1_	$a Cusimano, Maryann K. $t Tú eres mi te quiero. $l Spanish
430 _ _	$a You are my I love you
430 _ _	$a Tú eres mi te quiero
670 _ _	$a You are my I love you, 2013046
670 _ _	$a Cusimano, Maryann K. You are my I love you = Tú eres mi te quiero, 2012: ‡b cover (Tú eres mi te quiero)

All work and expression authority records include MARC fields 010, 040 and 670. The 010 includes the Library of Congress Control Number (LCCN), which serves as the unique identifier of the authorized access point. The 040 includes the National Union Catalog (NUC) symbols of the libraries that created or modified the record. For an RDA authority record prepared by an English-language cataloging agency, it also includes subfields $b eng and $e rda. The 670 includes the source on which the access point was based and the information found. This information may also be listed in other MARC fields with elements to which it applies.

Work and expression authority records include title or author/title authorized access points. Title authorized access points are given in MARC field 130, as shown in Figure 3.25. Personal author/title authorized access points are given in MARC field 100, as shown in Figures 3.26 and 3.27. Titles are recorded in subfield $t. Selections are listed in subfield $k. Other distinguishing characteristics of works and expressions are found in other subfields of MARC fields 100 and 130.

Languages that are part of expressions' authorized access points are found in subfield $l of MARC fields 100 and 130. The languages appear in the spelled out form in fields 100 and 130. As illustrated by the Maryann Cusimano's *You are My I Love You* example in Figure 3.27, language information is also given in MARC field 377. The three-letter language codes from *MARC Code List for Languages* are used instead of the spelled out forms of the languages for field 377.

Dates associated with works and expressions are given in subfield $f of MARC field 100. Dates are also in subfield $k and $l of MARC field 046. They are recorded according to standard ISO 8601. In Figure 3.25, for example, 2001 is given in fields 046 and 130 for the motion picture *Planet of the Apes*.

Authorized access points for motion pictures and television and radio programs are all qualified by their form of work. The *Planet of the Apes* example is qualified by *Motion picture*. That same term is also used in MARC field 380.

Authority records for works and expressions can all include variant names. Variant title access points are given in MARC field 430. Author/title variant access points are given in MARC field 400. The authority record for Maryann Cusimano's work (Figure 3.27) includes both author/title as well as title variant access points. The authorized author/title access point includes the original English language title, *You are My I Love You*. The variant author/title access point includes the Spanish title, *Tú eres mi te quiero*. Variant title access points are given for both the English and Spanish titles.

The relationships between works and expressions are given in authority records in MARC fields 500 and 530. RDA Chapters 24–26 cover these types of relationships. Relationship designators that are found in RDA Appendix J may be used in the subfield $i of these fields to identify different types of relationships. The authority record in Figure 3.25 includes examples of relationships between different works. The 2011 motion picture *Planet of the Apes* is an adaptation of Pierre Boulle's *Planète des singes*. It is a remake of the 1968 version of the motion picture. The FRBR term *Work* is part of the relationship information.

Conclusion

This chapter provided an introduction to the elements of authorized access points of persons, families, corporate bodies, works, and expressions. It explained how access points are constructed and how to interpret authority records. The process of maintaining consistency in how access points are created is important because it allows users to find and to identify that they have found the entity they were searching for. Authority records justify why a particular form of an access point was chosen and what it was based on. They also provide an understanding of the relationships among names, works, and expressions.

Exercise 3.1

Understanding Authority Records

Review each authority record. Answer the questions relating to the authority records.

010 _ _	$a n 79003974
040 _ _	$a ### $b eng $e rda $c ###
046 _ _	$f 18981129 $g 19631122
053 _0	$a PR6023.E926
100 1_	$a Lewis, C. S. $q (Clive Staples), $d 1898-1963
370 _ _	$a Belfast, Northern Ireland $b Oxford, England
373 _ _	$a Oxford University
373 _ _	$a Cambridge University
374 _ _	$a author $a scholar $a broadcaster
375 _ _	$a male
377 _ _	$a eng
400 1_	$a Lewis, Jack, $d 1898-1963
400 1_	$a Hamilton, Clive, $d 1898-1963
400 1_	$a Clerk, N. W., $d 1898-1963
400 1_	$a Lewis, Clive Staples, $d 1898-1963 $w nna
670 _ _	$a His Dymer, c1926.
670 _ _	$a His C.S. Lewis, his letters to children, c1985: $b CIP t.p. (C.S. Lewis) text (known as Jack Lewis; Clive Staples Lewis)
670 _ _	$a The voyage of the Dawn Treader, c2000: $b t.p. (C.S. Lewis) p. 3 of cover (b. in Belfast in 1898)
670 _ _	$a Wikipedia, WWW, June 15, 2011 $b (b. 29 Nov. 1898 in Belfast, Ireland; died 22 Nov. 1963 in Oxford, England; Irish-born British novelist, academic, medievalist, literary critic, essayist, lay theologian and Christian apologist; known to friends and family as Jack; on the English faculty at Oxford University and later at Cambridge University; novelist, scholar, broadcaster who wrote fantasy, science fiction, Christian apologetics, children's literature)

Questions

1. What was the month, day, and year of Lewis's birth?

2. What was the month, day, and year of Lewis's death?

3. Where was Lewis born? Where did he die?

4. What were Lewis's occupations?

From *The RDA Workbook: Learning the Basics of Resource Description and Access.*
Margaret Mering, Editor. Santa Barbara, CA: Libraries Unlimited. Copyright © 2014

5. What universities was Lewis associated with?

6. List Lewis's variant access points.

---

010 _ _	$a n 2002045864
040 _ _	$a ### $b eng $e rda $c ###
046 _ _	$f 19710828
100 1_	$a Sfar, Joann
370 _ _	$a Nice, France $e Paris, France
374 _ _	$a comics artist and creator
374 _ _	$a film director
375 _ _	$a male
377 _ _	$a fre
400 1_	$a Sfar, Joann, $d 1971-
670 _ _	$a Sfar, Joann. Little Vampire goes to school, 2003: $b ECIP data view (Joann Sfar)
670 _ _	$a Wikipedia, WWW, Sep. 28, 2011 $b (b. 28 August 1971 in Nice, France; French comics artist, comic book creator and film director)
670 _ _	$a :01 First Second, via WWW, Sep. 28, 2011 $b (lives in Paris with wife and children)

Questions

1. What was the month, day, and year of Sfar's birth?

2. Where was Sfar born?

3. Where does Sfar live?

4. What are Sfar's occupations?

5. What is Sfar's gender?

---

010 _ _	$a no2011026671
040 _ _	$a ### $b eng $e rda $c ###
046 _ _	$f 18800729 $g 19710725
100 1_	$a Meyers, Chief, $d 1880-1971
370 _ _	$a Riverside, Calif. $b San Bernardino, Calif.
373 _ _	$a New York Giants (Baseball team) $s 1909 $t 1915
373 _ _	$a Brooklyn Robins (Baseball team) $s 1916 $t 1917
373 _ _	$a Boston Braves (Baseball team) $s 1917 $t 1917
374 _ _	$a baseball player
375 _ _	$a male
400 1_	$a Meyers, John Tortes, $d 1880-1971

---

670 _ _	$a The glory of their times, 1984: $b page 170 (Chief Meyers)
670 _ _	$a Wikipedia, via WWW, February 17, 2011: $b (Chief Meyers; born John Tortes Meyers on July 29, 1880 in Riverside, California; died July 25, 1971 in San Bernardino, California; Major League Baseball player, 1909-1917; catcher for the New York Giants (1909-1915), Brooklyn Robins (1916-1917), and Boston Braves (1917))

Questions

1. What was the month, day, and year of Meyers's birth?

2. What was the month, day, and year of Meyers's death?

3. Where was Meyers born? Where did he die?

4. What years was Meyers a baseball player for the New York Giants?

5. What other baseball teams did Meyers play for?

6. What is Meyers's real name?

010 _ _	$a no2013001785
040 _ _	$a ### $b eng $e rda $c ###
046 _ _	$s 1923
110 2_	$a First-Plymouth Church (Lincoln, Neb.)
368 _ _	$a Church
370 _ _	$c U.S. $e Lincoln, Neb.
371 _ _	$a 2000 D Street $b Lincoln $c Neb. $d U.S. $e 68502 $s 1931 $v The art & architecture of First-Plymouth Church, 2011
372 _ _	$a Christianity $a Spirituality $2 lcsh $v First-Plymouth WWW site, about us page, viewed Nov. 27, 2012 $u http://www.firstplymouth .org/Pages/about_index.html
373 _ _	$a United Church of Christ $2 naf
377 _ _	$a eng
410 2_	$a First-Plymouth Congregational Church (Lincoln, Neb.)
410 2_	$a First-Plymouth Congregational Church UCC (Lincoln, Neb.)
670 _ _	$a The art & architecture of First-Plymouth Church, 2011: $b t.p. (First-Plymouth Church) p. 4 (First-Plymouth Congregational Church)
670 _ _	$a First-Plymouth Church WWW site, viewed Nov. 27, 2012 $b home page (First-Plymouth Church; part of the United Church of Christ) about us page (First-Plymouth Congregational Church; First-Plymouth Congregational Church UCC; merger of two congregations in 1923: First Congregational Church, organized Aug. 19, 1866, and Plymouth Congregational Church, organized 1887; new building at the corner of 20th and D Streets in Lincoln, Neb. dedicated on April 5, 1931)

678 _ _	$a First-Plymouth Church is a congregation of the United Church of Christ located at the corner of 20th and D Streets in Lincoln, Nebraska. The church was established in 1923 with the merger of First Congregational Church (organized 1866) and Plymouth Congregational Church (organized 1887).

Questions

1. What is the full address of First-Plymouth Church?

2. What year was the church established? What year was it dedicated?

3. Which churches merged to form First-Plymouth Church?

4. List the variant access points of First-Plymouth Church.

5. What church denomination is associated with First-Plymouth Church?

010 _ _	$a n 80123108
040 _ _	$a ### $b eng $e rda $c ###
046 _ _	$s 1962
053 _0	$a ML421.R64 $c Biography
110 2_	$a Rolling Stones
368 _ _	$a Rock groups $a Musical groups $2 lcsh
370 _ _	$e London, England
372 _ _	$a Rock music $a Blues (Music) $a Blues-rock music $a Rhythm and blues music $2 lcsh
410 2_	$a Stones (Musical group)
410 2_	$a The Rolling Stones
410 2_	$a The Stones (Musical group)
410 2_	$a Strolling Bones (Musical group)
410 2_	$a The Strolling Bones (Musical group)
500 1_	$i Group member: $a Jagger, Mick $w r
500 1_	$i Group member: $a Richards, Keith, $d 1943- $w r
670 _ _	$a Our own story, 1965, c1964.
670 _ _	$a L'agenda des Stones, 1982: $b t.p. (Stones) p. 3 (Rolling Stones)
670 _ _	$a Wikipedia, Nov. 3, 2012 $b (The Rolling Stones; English rock band formed in London in 1962; also known as The Stones, The Strolling Bones; origin: London, England; genres: Rock, blues, blues rock, rock and roll, rhythm and blues; years active: 1962-present; members: Mick Jagger; Keith Richards; Charlie Watts; Ronnie Wood; past members: Brian Jones; Ian Stewart; Bill Wyman; Mick Taylor; Dick Taylor)

Questions

1. What year did the musical group the Rolling Stones form?

2. Name two current members of the Rolling Stones.

3. What place is associated with the Rolling Stones?

4. List the Rolling Stones's variant access points.

5. What fields of activity are the Rolling Stones involved in?

010 _ _	$a n 2013000973
040 _ _	$a ### $b eng $e rda $c ###
046 _ _	$s 1895
100 3_	$a Cass (Family : $c Me.)
370 _ _	$c U.S. $e South Portland, Me.
376 _ _	$b Cass, Malcolm Walter, 1916-2008
667 _ _	$a SUBJECT USAGE: This heading is not valid for use as a subject; use a family name heading from LCSH.
670 _ _	$a NUCMC data from Maine Hist. Soc. for Its Collection, 1895-2003 $b (Cass family; residents of South Portland, Me., and other places in Maine; prominent members: Dr. Malcolm Walter Cass (1916-2008), optometrist and his wife Hildreth Estelle Edwards Cass (1918-2007)

Questions

1. What was the Cass family's place of residence?

2. What was the name of a prominent family member?

3. What source was used to establish the access point Cass (Family : Me.)?

010 _ _	$a n 2012051678
040 _ _	$a ### $b eng $e rda $c ###
046 _ _	$s 20100719 $t 20100723
111 2_	$a International Conference on Spectral Geometry $d (2010 : $c Dartmouth College)
411 2_	$a Conference on Spectral Geometry, International $d (2010 : $c Dartmouth College)
670 _ _	$a Spectral geometry, 2012: $b ECIP t.p. (July 19-23, 2010, Dartmouth College, Dartmouth, New Hampshire) galley (International Conference on Spectral Geometry)

Questions

1. Which days in 2010 was the conference held?

2. At what institution was the conference held?

From *The RDA Workbook: Learning the Basics of Resource Description and Access.* Margaret Mering, Editor. Santa Barbara, CA: Libraries Unlimited. Copyright © 2014

010 _ _	$a n 2013003177
040 _ _	$a ### $b eng $e rda $c ###
100 1_	$a Cather, Willa, $d 1873-1947. $t Works. $k Selections
400 1_	$a Cather, Willa, $d 1873-1947. $t April twilights and other poems
670 _ _	$a April twilights and other poems, 2013: $b CIP t.p. verso and data sheet (This edition reprints Willa Cather's 1903 collection of poems (called April Twilights) along with the additional poems she added in 1923 (in a collection she called April twilights and other poems). In addition it includes many uncollected and previously unpublished poems, along with a selection of Cather's letters that are relevant to her poetry from The selected letters of Willa Cather, edited by Stout and Jewell and published 2013 by Knopf))

Questions

1. Works. Selections is used for publications that include more than one form of writing. *April Twilights and Other Poems* includes:

   a. Poems
   b. Short stories
   c. Correspondence
   d. Novels

Quick Guide to RDA Authority Records

Selected MARC terms, tags, and subfields in authority records for persons, families, corporate bodies, conferences, works, and expressions

Persons

MARC Term	MARC Tag	MARC Subfields	RDA
Special Coded Dates	046 _ _	$f Birth date $g Death date	9.3.2 9.3.3
Name of Person	100 1_ Forename only 100 0_ Surname	$a Personal name $c Titles of person	Chapter 9
Other Attributes of Person	368 _ _	$d Title of person $s Start period	$d Dates $q Fuller form of name	$t End period	9.4 9.6
Associated Place	370 _ _	$a Place of birth $b Place of death $c Associated country	$e Place of residence $f Other associated place	9.8, 9.9, 9.10, 9.11
Address	371 _ _	$a Address $b City $c Intermediate jurisdiction $d Country	$e Postal code $m Electronic mail address $s Start period $t End period	9.12
Field of Activity	372 _ _	$a Field of activity $s Start period	$t End period	9.15
Associated Group	373 _ _	$a Associated Group $s Start period	$t End period	9.13
Occupation	374 _ _	$a Occupation $s Start period	$t End period	9.16
Gender	375 _ _	$a Gender $s Start period	$t End period	9.7

MARC Term	MARC Tag	MARC Subfields	RDA
Associated Language	377 _ _	$a Language code	9.14
Fuller Form of Personal Name	378 _ _	$q Fuller form of name	9.5
Variant Access Point	400 1_ Forename Only 400 0_ Surname	$a Personal name $c Titles of Person	$d Dates $q Fuller form of name	Chapter 9
Relationships	500 _ _ Personal name 510 _ _ Corporate name 511 _ _ Meeting name		Section 9 (Chapters 29-32)
Source Data Found	670 _ _	$a Source citation $b Information found	
Biographical/ Historical Data	678 _ _	$a Biographical data	9.17

Families

MARC Term	MARC Tag	MARC Subfields	RDA
Special Coded Dates	046 _ _	$s Start period $t End period	10.4
Name of Family	100 3_	$a Family name $c Titles and other words associated with a name $d Dates $g Prominent family member	Chapter 10
Associated Place	370 _ _	$c Associated country $e Place of residence $f Other associated place	10.5
Family information	376 _ _	$a Type of family $b Prominent family member $c Hereditary title $s Start period $t End period	10.3 10.6 10.7
Variant Access Point	400 3_	$a Family name $c Titles and other words $d Dates $g Prominent family member	Chapter 10
Relationships	500 _ _ Personal name 510 _ _ Corporate name 511 _ _ Meeting name		Section 9 (Chapters 29-32)
Note Concerning Use of Access Point	667 _ _	$a Nonpublic general note	
Source Data Found	670 _ _	$a Source citation $b Information found	
Biographical/ Historical Data	678 _ _	$a Biographical data	10.8

Corporate Bodies

MARC Term	MARC Tag	MARC Subfields	RDA
Special Coded Dates	046 _ _	$s Start period $t End period	11.4
Name of Corporate Body	110 1_ Jurisdiction name 110 0_ Name in direct order	$a Corporate name or jurisdiction name $c Subordinate unit	Chapter 11
Other Attributes of Corporate Body	368 _ _	$a Type of corporate body $d Type of jurisdiction $c Other jurisdiction $s Start period $t End period	11.7
Associated Place	370 _ _	$a Associated country $e Place of headquarters $f Other associated place $s Start period $t End period	11.3.3
Address	371 _ _	$a Address $b City $c Intermediate jurisdiction $d Country $e Postal code $m Electronic mail address $s Start period $t End period	11.9
Field of Activity	372 _ _	$a Field of activity $s Start period $t End period	11.10
Associated Group	373 _ _	$a Associated group $s Start period $t End period	11.5
Associated Language	377 _ _	$a Language code	11.8

MARC Term	MARC Tag	MARC Subfields	RDA
Variant Access Point	410 1_ Jurisdiction name 410 2_ Name in direct order	$a Corporate name or jurisdiction name $b Subordinate unit $d Dates $q Fuller form of name	Chapter 11
Relationships	500 _ _ Personal name 510 _ _ Corporate name 511 _ _ Meeting name	—	Section 9 (Chapters 29-32)
Source Data Found	670 _ _	$a Source citation $b Information found	
Biographical/ Historical Data	678 _ _	$a Biographical data	11.11

Conferences

MARC Term	MARC Tag	MARC Subfields	RDA
Special Coded Dates	046 _ _	$s Start period $t End period	11.4
Name of Meeting/ Conference	111 1_ Jurisdiction name 111 2_ Name in direct order	$a Meeting/Jurisdiction name $c Location of meeting $d Date of meeting	Chapter 11
Other Designations of Corporate Body	368 _ _	$a Type of corporate body $d Type of jurisdiction $c Other designation $s Start period $t End period	11.7
Associated Place	370 _ _	$c Associated country $e Location $f Other associated place $s Start period $t End period	11.3.2
Address	371 _ _	$a Address $b City $c Intermediate jurisdiction $d Country $e Postal code $m Electronic mail address $s Start period $t End period	11.9
Field of Activity	372 _ _	$a Field of activity $s Start period	$t End period 11.10
Associated Group	373 _ _	$a Associated group $s Start period	$t End period 11.5
Associated Language	377 _ _	$a Language code	11.8

MARC Term	MARC Tag	MARC Subfields	RDA
Variant Access Point	411 1_ Jurisdiction name 411 2_ Name in direct order	$a Meeting/Jurisdiction name $c Location of meeting $d Date of meeting	Chapter 11
Relationships	500 _ _ Personal name 510 _ _ Corporate name 511 _ _ Meeting name		Section 9 (Chapters 29-32)
Source Data Found	670 _ _	$a Source citation $b Information found	
Biographical/ Historical Data	678 _ _	$a Historical data	11.11

Works			
MARC Term	**MARC Tag**	**MARC Subfields**	**RDA**
Special Coded Dates	046 _ _	$s Start period $t End period	6.4
Authorized Access Point/ Preferred Name	100 1_ Forename 100 0_ Surname	$a Personal name $c Titles of person $d Dates of person $q Fuller form of name $d Date of work $k Form subheading/selections $t Title of work	Chapter 9 Chapter 6
Preferred Title	130 _0	$a Title of work $f Date of work $k Form subheading	Chapter 6
Associated Place	370 _ _	$g Place of origin of work	6.5
Form of Work	380 _ _	$a Form of work	6.3
Other Distinguishing Characteristics of Work	381 _ _	$a Other distinguishing characteristics of work	6.6
Variant Access Point	400 1_ Forename 400 0_ Surname	$a Personal name $c Titles of person $d Dates of person $q Fuller form of name $d Date of work $k Form subheading/selections $t Title of work	Chapter 9 Chapter 6
Variant Access Point	430 _0	$a Title of work $f Date of work $k Form subheading	Chapter 9 Chapter 6
Source Data Found	670 _ _	$a Source citation $b Information found	

Expressions

MARC Term	MARC Tag	MARC Subfields	RDA
Special Coded Dates	046 _ _	$s Start period $t End period	6.10
Authorized Access Point/ Preferred Name	100 1_ Forename 100 0_ Surname	$a Personal name $c Titles of person $d Dates of person $q Fuller form of name $k Form subheading/selections $l Language $t Title of work	Chapter 9 Chapter 6
Preferred Title	130 _0	$a Title of work $f Date of work $k Form subheading $l Language	Chapter 9 Chapter 6
Associated Place	370 _ _	$g Place of origin of work	6.5
Associated Language	377 _ _	$a Language of expression	6.11
Other Designations Associated with Expression	381 _ _	$a Other distinguishing characteristics	6.12
Variant Access Point	400 1_ Forename 400 0_ Surname	$a Personal name $c Titles of person $d Dates of person $q Fuller form of name $k Form subheading/selections $l Language $t Title of work	Chapter 9 Chapter 6
Variant Access Point	430 _0	$a Title of work $f Date of work $k Form subheading $l Language	Chapter 9 Chapter 6
Source Data Found	670 _ _	$a Source citation $b Information found	

4

Implementing RDA into Your Library and Catalog

Casey Kralik

Each library is on a different path to *Resource Description and Access* (RDA). While many libraries are aware of the Library of Congress's implementation of RDA on March 31, 2013, they do not have a plan for incorporating RDA into their own cataloging practices. When creating an implementation plan, one of the biggest challenges is knowing where to begin.

The previous two chapters focused on RDA changes to bibliographic and authority records. This chapter shifts to implementing these changes in our catalogs by setting up a suggested timeline. Establishing a timeline will provide a practical and realistic approach to mapping out the various tasks needed for a successful change. The facets of the timeline can be customized to fit your local needs, and not all of them are required for an implementation plan. Each section of this chapter concludes with a list of questions that can help you formulate your own local RDA timeline.

Goals for Chapter 4:
- Map a plan for implementation.
- Introduce RDA to staff; prepare the budget.
- Decide local practices and update your integrated library system (ILS).
- Train and educate staff and patrons.
- Prepare for the future.

The timeline in Figure 4.1 shows implementation in three phases. The first phase includes introducing RDA, mapping goals, assessing the staff and catalog, and planning a budget. The second phase involves working with your ILS and vendors, setting up local decisions and practices, and training technical services staff. Finally, the third phase focuses on training public services staff and preparing for future changes. The amount of time spent on each phase will

Figure 4.1
Timeline for RDA Implementation

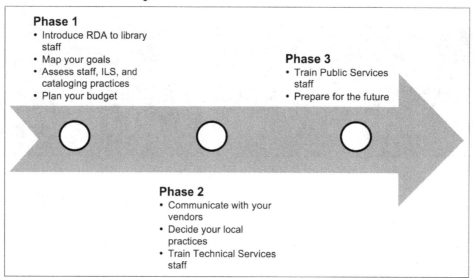

be determined by many things, including your library's setting, number of staff, staff time, and staff knowledge of implementation.

Phase 1a: Introduce RDA to Library Staff

The first step in phase 1 begins with a plan on how to introduce RDA to the library staff and administration. Consider the audience and what new knowledge will be of most benefit to them. The introduction can include topics such as RDA terminology and definitions, RDA as a content standard (as previously discussed in Chapter 1), and the major differences between *Anglo-American Cataloguing Rules*, Second Edition (AACR2) and RDA. In addition, a visual demonstration of how RDA records appear in a catalog that has integrated the new records would be beneficial. Finally, address questions and concerns and let staff know that an implementation timeline and process will be formed.

According to the Joint Steering Committee (JSC) for Development of RDA's *Frequently Asked Questions* on library system changes, "it is hoped that eventually library systems and OPACs will evolve to take full advantage of the data created using RDA, with its underlying FRBR structure of work, expression, manifestation, and item. These changes will improve the ease and effectiveness with which users are able to find, identify, and obtain the resources they require" (6.3).

Questions

- What information will be covered in the introduction of RDA?
  - Will RDA and *Functional Requirements for Bibliographic Records* (FRBR) be covered?

- ○ Will the history of the cataloging codes and the reasons for the changes made in RDA be shared?
  - ○ Will the new or changed elements found in bibliographic records (e.g., loss of the general material designation [GMD]) be a focus?
  - ○ Will examples of RDA and FRBR from other library catalogs be shown?
  - ○ Will a justification for spending time and money on training and implementation of RDA be included?
- Who will be included in the audience?
  - ○ Will there be separate presentations based on the audience?
  - ○ Will there be one for the entire staff, including administration?
  - ○ Will there be several small sessions with select individuals?
  - ○ Will there be a presentation to the library board?
- How will questions and feedback be addressed?
  - ○ What kinds of questions are expected from library staff?
  - ○ What are some ways that questions can be addressed prior to the presentation?
  - ○ How will staff be positively motivated toward these changes?
- Will the plan for implementation be introduced at this time?

Phase 1b: Map Your Goals

The next step in the implementation of RDA is to map out goals for the transition. Goals should be specific and focus on something that is measurable. In addition, goals should be challenging, but attainable, and include an end date. RDA implementation will be a group effort that will need to be designed to include variables such as staff time and knowledge as well as factors outside your control such as ILS vendors.

Examples of Goals

- In one year's time, the library catalog will support and reflect the changes made due to the implementation of RDA.
- By the end of the second year, all original bibliographic and authority records entered into the catalog will follow RDA standards.
- By the end of phase 1, communicate with individual library staff members concerning their priorities for implementation.

Questions

- Who will create the goals?
- Will all library staff and administration be given an opportunity to provide input and/or feedback related to the goals?

- What are the library's goals for implementation of RDA?
- How will the goals be measured?
- Will the library staff set several large goals but break them down into smaller short-term goals?
- How will goals be prioritized and communicated?
- What will be the beginning and end dates for implementation?
- Who will need to be involved with implementation?

Phase 1c: Assess Staff, ILS, and Cataloging Practices

Next, perform an assessment of the staff, ILS, and cataloging practices. For assessment of staff, create an inventory indicating each staff member's potential level of involvement with the RDA changes, ranging from minimal to full. Provide a description of their duties and experience with bibliographic and authority records. To determine the cost, estimate how many hours each staff member will spend on implementation and multiply that by their hourly rate of pay. Figure 4.2 shows an example of a library's staff assessment. Worksheet 4.1 provides a blank form to perform an assessment of your library.

Public services staff will need to understand and be included in discussions concerning the changes RDA will have on the catalog. Explain the impact of RDA on both catalog search results and display of new or changed elements in bibliographic records. Find out how the changes will affect their use of the catalog and make decisions based on their needs. This knowledge will guide changes to the display and indexing of new MAchine-Readable Cataloging (MARC) fields in the catalog.

Assessment of the catalog system and cataloging practices is also needed to determine the extent of the changes needed for RDA. Investigate if the catalog has the latest version of the software. If it does not, plan for upgrades, especially if they include making changes for RDA. Finally, take note of local cataloging practices and find out how many RDA records are being discovered by copy catalogers. Determine the course of action taken by catalogers when encountering these records.

Questions

Staff

- How many staff members will be involved in implementing RDA?
- In what ways will staff time spent on implementation affect daily tasks and other projects? Will work have to be redistributed?
- What are the time requirements for each staff member to spend on learning RDA?
- Will expectations be formalized and prioritized for staff?

Figure 4.2
Factoring Staff Time and Cost Example

Merrick Public Library				
In one year, the library will have implemented RDA and estimates 1,750 work hours for the project.				
Staff Name	Title & Duties	Role/Involvement with RDA	Project Hours	Cost*
Mikela	Reference Librarian; catalog searching	Moderate; testing before and after RDA changes made to catalog	250 hours	$15/hour = $3,750
Max	Cataloging Librarian; creates, imports copy and original bibliographic records	Full; studies RDA instructions, edits RDA incoming records, creates records in RDA	700 hours	$18/hour = $12,600
Nora	Systems Administrator; proficient in making changes to system formats, works with vendor	Full; responsible for bibliographic and authority format changes including display and indexing configurations, works with vendor customer support	500 hours	$20/hour = $10,000
Erik	Circulation Manager; catalog searching	Minimal; testing before and after RDA changes made to catalog	200 hours	$10/hour = $2000
Daniel	Library Director; plans budget, works with vendor	Minimal; plans budget, works with vendor	100 hours	$25/hour = $2500

* Earnings per hour × project hours

ILS

- Is the catalog ready to support the changes for RDA?
- Has the vendor provided updates to accommodate the changes for RDA? If so, have the updates been applied to the ILS system?
- Which library staff members have the administrative rights to implement the changes to the ILS?
- How many staff members make and lead decisions based on RDA changes to the ILS? Do they have the RDA knowledge to back their decisions?

Cataloging Practices

- Do the current cataloging practices allow RDA records to be edited and brought into the catalog?
- Until the MARC-related changes are made, will RDA records be imported into the catalog? If not, what will be done with the affected materials?
- How many staff members will be involved with the decisions on local practices for the changes from RDA?

Phase 1d: Plan Your Budget

Planning a budget is an essential step for a successful implementation, as it will take time and money. From staff time spent on training to money spent on a subscription to the RDA Toolkit, calculate and plan for both seen and unforeseen expenses.

Access to RDA Instructions

There are several options for accessing the RDA instructions. One is to subscribe to the online RDA Toolkit, which has various pricing models. In addition, a free 30-day trial to the RDA Toolkit is offered.

A print version, *RDA: Resource Description and Access*, is also available. A new loose-leaf publication is currently scheduled for release in 2013. A third resource, with the working title *Essential RDA* and slated for publication in both print and as an eBook, is noted to be "a companion to RDA with a foundation of RDA basic instructions and core elements" (Hennely 2013, under "Essential RDA").

When making a decision on how to access the RDA instructions, consider the pros and cons of online versus print resources. Cost, updating options, and number of staff needing access will all factor in toward the purchase.

Training and Education Costs

Several factors affect the cost and time for training of technical and public services staff. Factor in the overall time needed to train based on the number of staff. Their skill level (consider that they come from a combination of experience and education) will also determine time needed for training. Factor a loss of productivity to their regular duties due to the time spent in training.

Questions

- How will catalogers access the RDA instructions?
- If the library opts for an online subscription to the RDA Toolkit, which option will be purchased? How many users will need access?

- If RDA in print is purchased, how much will be factored in for the cost of updates?
- Are there costs associated with updating the catalog system for the RDA changes?
- Are there additional costs for updating the bibliographic and authority records for RDA?
- What costs will come from investment of staff time in updating the system or facilitating the changes?
- What costs are associated with training staff (both technical and public services)? Will this include a travel budget if staff members need to attend nonlocal workshops and conferences?

Phase 2a: Communicate with Your Vendors

In response to the question on the effect of RDA on an integrated library system, the JSC's *Frequently Asked Questions* says, "the Outreach Group and the RDA Project Manager see the ILS vendors as major stakeholders in the RDA process and will continue to inform them when important RDA documents are available for comment, and keep them up-to-date regarding progress in RDA's online development" (6.2).

ILS Vendor Communication and Support

Communication with the library's ILS vendor is key to preparing the catalog for implementation of RDA. The vendor should be aware of the changes needed for RDA and address them with the library. If the vendor has not communicated this information, the library should take some responsibility for finding this information. Keeping up on documentation or news releases about how and when the ILS vendor will make implementation happen is critical. Check out their website, blogs, newsletters, emails, and any other forms of communication they may have with their customers.

Networking with other users that have the same system may also be helpful, including the ILS vendor's email discussion lists. In addition, the vendor's website may offer community forums or archived questions where information may have been shared on implementation of RDA changes. Finally, attending user group meetings will provide opportunities for face-to-face discussion about other users' implementation experiences.

Changes to the ILS

Communication with the ILS vendor about new MARC fields for bibliographic and authority data may result in several paths for implementation. Some vendors may have already started to prepare for RDA and have planned related updates to the system. If there are planned updates to be implemented by the vendor, determine the extent of those changes and if they include changes to record display and indexing. If few or no changes are expected from an update by the vendor, decide who in the library will be responsible for making the necessary changes to the ILS. The changes made to the catalog display and indexing of the new MARC fields will depend entirely on local decisions made by the library. In addition, the catalog will need reindexing as changes are made, or if RDA records have been imported between system updates, to reflect the changes. Finally, keep abreast of the ILS vendor's plans to apply the *Functional Requirements for Bibliographic Records* (FRBR) to the catalog.

Bibliographic and Authority Records

Once RDA changes have been applied to the system, investigate the RDA implementation plans of bibliographic and authority record providers. Whether imported records come from vendors such as Baker & Taylor, eBrary, OCLC, or via a Z39.50 protocol, find out how and to what extent each provider has implemented RDA or if RDA records are added to their database. In addition, if authority work is outsourced to a vendor, talk with the vendor to see if RDA has been implemented. Because RDA implementation has resulted in a large number of changed authority records and their corresponding access points in bibliographic records, ask the vendor how they plan to distribute the large numbers of changed records.

If the library contributes records to a shared database, consider the RDA implementation policies of the database. For example, according to the *OCLC RDA Policy Statement,* which went into effect on March 31, 2013, contributing libraries may continue to add original records using AACR2 to the database after March 31, 2013, but OCLC "duplicate records are contrary to WorldCat policy and hinder the work of the cooperative." It further states, "separate records for the same manifestation entered for different cataloging codes (e.g., AACR2 and RDA) are not allowed" (OCLC, under "Effective March 31, 2013").

Federated and Discovery Systems

Similar to communicating with the ILS vendor, speak with the federated or discovery system vendor concerning adding the new MARC fields, the impact on display and indexing, and future plans for FRBR. In addition, determine how the catalog is mapped to the federated or discovery system. Do the fields match up? Is the display and indexing of each new field the same between all of the systems your library uses (e.g., the staff interface, online public access catalog [OPAC], and discovery layer)? Once changes have been made, perform a few test searches in both systems. Do you get the same results? If not, how will it impact the user?

Questions

ILS Vendor Communication and Support

- What methods of communication do vendors have with the library?
- How do vendors communicate important changes such as planned updates for RDA to the catalog system?
- What kinds of support systems do vendors provide and/or facilitate?

Changes to the ILS

- Who will make the changes to the catalog system?
- What does the vendor provide in updates to the catalog system? New MARC fields? Changes to display and/or index settings?
- Once the library has determined who will make the changes to the system or oversee the changes, the library may have an option to customize the new fields. What decisions will your library make initially on which fields are displayed and indexed?
- How much time will your library allot to each staff member to either make or oversee the changes?

Bibliographic and Authority Records

- Where do library staff find bibliographic and authority records for import into the catalog system?
- Have these providers communicated their implementation plans for RDA?
- If records come from multiple outside sources, which standards of practice are followed when creating these records? For example, do those creating the records follow the Library of Congress–Program for Cooperative Cataloging Policy Statements (LC-PCC PS)? How much of this will affect the consistency of the records?

Federated and Discovery Systems

- How are the MARC fields mapped from your ILS system to your federated or discovery system?
- Does the federated or discovery system display the new RDA fields? Are they indexed?
- Which library staff makes changes to the federated or discovery system's fields?

Phase 2b: Decide Your Local Practices

After the new MARC fields have been added to the ILS, staff will be ready to discuss changes related to its display and indexing. These discussions will lead to local decisions for addressing public and technical services' needs, managing a hybrid catalog, and documenting policies and procedures.

Public Services

Communication between public services and technical services remains essential when making local RDA decisions, especially those impacting the display of RDA content in your OPAC or the indexing of new MARC fields in your catalog. Base your local decisions on the needs of your patrons. Consider how library users interact with your online catalog, and determine how the RDA changes may affect their search and discovery process. For example, what decisions need to be made to help a user identify a DVD of *My Ántonia*? Which parts of the bibliographic record identify the resource as Willa Cather's *My Ántonia*? What does the user look for when determining the format of the resource—in other words, how do they know this is a DVD and not a VHS tape or a downloadable video? Exercise 4.1 presents examples of DVD records in AACR2 and RDA. Have public services staff circle the parts of each bibliographic record that help identify the resource as a DVD. Compare the AACR2 and RDA records. What are the differences? What are the similarities?

Operating in a Hybrid Catalog

Many libraries are already operating a hybrid catalog that includes resources cataloged according to RDA, AACR2, and even earlier cataloging codes. However, it is still necessary to evaluate and adjust your implementation plans. Concerns about having a hybrid catalog were addressed in a report of the PCC Post-Implementation Hybrid Bibliographic Records Guidelines Task Group, which stated, "The U.S. national libraries testing of RDA determined that RDA records could co-exist successfully with non-RDA records" (2013, under "Summary"). What is the impact of the hybrid catalog on the searching habits of the user?

Your catalog will have a mixture of new and old MARC fields, which supports both AACR2 and RDA records. Those cataloging at your library will continue to add AACR2 records, but will begin to see and add more RDA records. The PCC report leads by example for catalogers and other policymakers. The *OCLC RDA Policy Statement* does address hybrid records and machine manipulation of existing records. It notes that it will follow the report of the PCC Post-Implementation Hybrid Bibliographic Records Guidelines Task Group. OCLC's policy also addresses the option to enhance non-RDA records to RDA. Libraries may consider options for converting legacy records to RDA standards.

Authority Records and Split Files

As discussed in Chapter 3, some access points will be constructed differently than they were following AACR2 rules. Investigate how the system will handle authorization of access points when RDA authority and bibliographic

Figure 4.3
Examples of Split Files

Catalog Browse Results when Searching for Walser H. Allen		
Access Point	**Hits**	**Cataloging Guidelines**
Allen, W. W.	1	
Allen, Waldo M.	1	
Allen, Walser H., 1898-1973.	1	RDA
Allen, Walser H., 1898-1973, $e author.	1	RDA
Allen, Walser Haddon, 1898-	2	AACR2
Allen, Walter.	3	

Catalog Browse Results when Searching for John Sandford		
Access Point	**Hits**	**Cataloging Guidelines**
Sandford, Jeremy.	1	
Sandford, John.	20	
Sandford, John, 1801 or 2-1873.	1	
Sandford, John, 1944 Feb. 23-	2	AACR2
Sandford, John, 1944 February 23- $e author.	1	RDA
Sandford, John, 1944 Jan. 1-	3	
Sandford, John B.		

Catalog Browse Results when Searching for Nebraska State Department of Health		
Access Point	**Hits**	**Cataloging Guidelines**
Nebraska Dental Association.	3	
Nebraska. Department of Health.	1	RDA
Nebraska. Department of Labor.	1	RDA
Nebraska. Dept. of Administrative Services.	1	
--------------------------------Intervening Screens--------------------------------		
Nebraska. Dept. of Environmental Quality.	2	
Nebraska. Dept. of Health.	3	AACR2
Nebraska. Dept. of Labor.	1	AACR2
Nebraska. Dept. of Motor Vehicles.	1	

records are integrated into the catalog. Unless new corresponding authority records have been added, any changes to the old forms of access points in bibliographic records will cause a break in the cross-reference structures. If new and revised authority files are added by staff, consider two possibilities for the catalog. The first possibility includes not updating the old forms of access points in bibliographic records as the revised authority records are added to the catalog. This will result in a split file for access points. Not all revised authority records will require changes to the existing access points because some will remain the same as they were in AACR2. The second possibility includes retroactively making changes to the old forms of access points as revised authority records are imported.

Furthermore, the addition of relationship designators to access points will cause split files unless the catalog can ignore the subfield $e with the designator terms. Figure 4.3 illustrates access points that have been split because the catalog has bibliographic records with both the AACR2 and the RDA forms of the names.

Technical Services

Technical services catalogers will face many decisions when editing and creating RDA records. Once the transition to RDA has been completed, a major decision will be whether imported AACR2 records will be converted to RDA or accepted as is. While the RDA instructions state which elements are core, core-if, transcribed, and so on, there are many options that allow for a cataloger's judgment. Previous discussions with public services staff will determine the choices made concerning such things as capitalization, the statement of responsibility, publication dates, and relationship designators.

Documentation and Best Practices

As local decisions are made and practices are established, document the reasons behind the decisions. Formulate policy and practice statements that are based on the staff's testing, discussions, and training. In addition to the policy and practice statements, step-by-step procedures for both copy cataloging and original cataloging staff should be documented. Decide what quality checks need to be in place for MARC records purchased from vendors.

Questions

Public Services

- Should all of the new MARC fields display in the OPAC? If fields are suppressed, what impact will that have on the user tasks of find, identify, and select?
- Which new fields should be indexed and made searchable?
- How do library staff and patrons search the catalog?
- How will the loss of certain elements such as the GMD affect identification of materials in the catalog? Can the 33x and/or other fields be used to fill in this gap?

Operating in a Hybrid Catalog

- How will a hybrid catalog (with both AACR2 and RDA records) impact a user's discovery of resources?
- Will some conversion of AACR2 records to RDA be addressed?
- How will the user's identification of materials be affected by seeing some of the records with GMDs and some without?
- How will having a mixture of MARC fields 260 and 264 in the catalog affect staff and patron interactions with the record?
- Some libraries have citation tools integrated with their catalog (e.g., Endnote). What implications will the changes for RDA have on how third-party tools are used?

Authority Records and Split Files

- How will having split authority files affect browse searching and linking of access points?

- Will current access points in the catalog be updated to reflect the RDA changes? If yes, how will that be done?
- Have portions of access points been omitted knowing that changes would be coming?
- Will there be RDA access points in AACR2 bibliographic records? Or vice versa? What effect will this have on searching?

Technical Services

- What guidelines will be established for copy catalogers to follow? Will different guidelines be established for different sources of bibliographic records?
- What guidelines will be established for original catalogers?
- What decisions will be made on relationship designators? Will they be retained? Will terms or codes be used?
- How will capitalization in a bibliographic record be treated? Will catalogers follow the International Standard Bibliographic Description (ISBD) punctuation when creating a new record?
- Will catalogers convert non-ISBD records to ISBD before importing them into the catalog?
- Will catalogers convert MARC field 260 to field 264? How much conversion of AACR2 records will take place when bringing in new records? Will catalogers convert the legacy records found in the catalog?
- Will the catalog list all the statements of responsibility in the subfield $c of the 245 MARC field? Will it include access points for all the creators listed in the statement of responsibility?
- What choices will be made concerning the other options in RDA?
- Who will be responsible for quality control?

Phase 2c: Train Technical Services Staff

Getting Started

The length of time spent on training technical services staff will depend largely on the number of staff and their experience and education. In addition, the type of library, its users, and its collection will drive the clock on implementation. For some libraries, it may mean in-depth training for original cataloging of special formats; for other libraries, where everything is outsourced, it will mean communication with ILS, MARC record, and authority record vendors.

Catalogers will need training on everything from recognizing an RDA record to creating an RDA record from a blank form. At the basic level, catalogers will need to be able to identify aspects of an RDA record. In addition, catalogers may encounter incomplete RDA records and hybrid AACR2/RDA records. Catalogers will need training related to upgrading incomplete records or making edits to inaccuracies in an RDA record. Who will be responsible for this level of editing and creating new records at the library? To what degree will the catalogers receive training?

Access to RDA

An integral part of training will be accessing and learning RDA from either the print edition or from a subscription to the RDA Toolkit. Whichever form is chosen, training will include a period of time devoted to exploring the navigation and search features of the RDA Toolkit or the index and table of contents of the print version.

If your library chooses a subscription to the toolkit, the training should include learning about other resources within the toolkit, such as workflows, crosswalks, and FRBR entities (see Quick Guide 1.4). The toolkit is updated bimonthly and integrated with the LC-PCC PS, which are available in the toolkit for free. There is also a free RDA Toolkit Essentials webinar offered every other month.

Web Resources for Training

The Library of Congress's RDA: Resource Description & Access Training Materials website offers a great place to start looking for training materials. Not only are there many community resources and documents available, but there are also webcasts, modules, exercises, and examples under the Training portion, all of which are free. These resources have been updated with the latest changes that resulted from the Library of Congress's testing. Although the training materials are meant for LC staff, many libraries that follow LC's policies will want to explore this website, especially if they import LC-created records into their catalog.

Similarly, the Program for Cooperative Cataloging (PCC) has an RDA Training website. There are links to programs, workshops, task groups, interim policies, and best practices. Documentation found on this website is rich with authority data and implementation guidelines.

Continuing Education

Workshops are also offered by professional associations. The Association for Library Collections and Technical Services (ALCTS), LYRASIS, and other associations and academic institutions offer online and face-to-face classes for a fee. There is a range of topics and fees depending on what is offered. Members often get a discount. The ALCTS Online Learning website, for example, lists upcoming web courses and workshops. In addition, their Webinar Archive website lists free webinars arranged by date while their YouTube channel, ALCTS Continuing Education, hosts original broadcasts three months after they were presented.

Cataloging Community Support

Consider organizing a local group of colleagues to practice creating RDA records. The Nebraska RDA Practice Group, comprised of technical services librarians from throughout the state, met monthly to explore and discuss various RDA topics (Gardner and Bernstein 2012). A local cataloging community group is a great way to communicate and connect on implementation questions, policies, and practices. If no such group exists in your area, consider starting one and inviting your regional colleagues.

From discussion lists to social media, the cataloging community provides generous support for RDA training. There are many good resources that can provide further information about what you have heard on a webinar or found on a website. Email discussion lists also provide current information on RDA. Some examples are Autocat, OCLC-Cat, PCCList, and RDA-L.

Finally, blogs and other social media avenues are increasing in activity with posts and interactions from community members. Social media sites such as Facebook and LinkedIn enable users to post questions, comments, and resources.

Questions

Getting Started

- Who will be responsible for in-house training of original and copy catalogers?
- Will training be customized to the cataloger?

Access to RDA

- If the RDA Toolkit is used, will training include time learning its structure, the workflows, the mappings, and other important aspects?
- If the print version is used, will time be spent on using the index and table of contents, and identifying the sections most often used for cataloging at your library?

Web Resources for Training

- Will training include listening to webcasts, performing exercises, and reading notes provided by the Library of Congress about RDA?
- What other web resources will be used?
- Will these be shared and discussed in your library?

Continuing Education

- How much education does the cataloging staff need for RDA?
- Will web courses be pursued?

- Are there face-to-face classes being taught in your area that staff members can attend?

Cataloging Community Support

- Does your library have a community of catalogers that communicates regularly about RDA? If there is not, is there someone who can lead such a community?
- Does your library association or group offer face-to-face workshops on RDA?
- Will a web community better support your catalogers' needs?
- Will your catalogers check in with social media such as blogs, Facebook, and LinkedIn to follow discussions and questions about RDA?
- Will your catalogers sign up for email discussion lists or search their archived posts for answers to RDA questions?

Phase 3a: Train Public Services Staff

The level and degree of training of the public services staff will be based on a couple of factors. First, use the staff assessment to determine the baseline of how much training is needed and for how many people. Many web presentations are available that examine portions of introducing RDA and giving the basics. The JSC's Presentations on RDA website has a lengthy listing of presentations by people connected with the development of RDA.

Phase 1 included an investigation of how the catalog was searched and used. Examine again how the changes for RDA that have been made affect searching and how things can be found in the catalog successfully. If public services staff were not included in the earlier testing, give them an overview of the changes that will appear in the local catalog. The focus should be on the following specific bibliographic changes:

- 33x fields, loss of GMD
- 264 field(s), 260 replacement
- Transcription
- Relationship designators
- Hybrid catalog/records

The appearance of the bibliographic record can vary from system to system, especially because individual libraries can make their own customizations. Many libraries have decided that the placement or suppression of certain MARC fields will help lead to the successful implementation of the changes for RDA.

Using their knowledge of what data was used for identification prior to the implementation of RDA, have public services staff members search different formats to illustrate the changes. How does staff interact with the search functions, search results list, filters, and any other narrowing tools such as facets? How do they respond to the changes that have been made in bibliographic records?

Based on their feedback, what changes still need to be made? Be prepared to explain the components of an RDA record and what they may or may not replace in an AACR2 record. If it has not already been communicated, or if a refresher is needed, go over the importance of and need for the new cataloging standard and the benefits of moving toward a new framework.

Additionally, find out how the library users interact with the catalog, either by getting direct feedback or indirect feedback via public services staff. This may have also happened to some degree in testing. Getting public services staff to embrace the changes will show the library's ultimate success in completing its implementation goals.

Questions

- In preparation for training of public services staff, what kinds of training resources would be helpful? Are there web presentations available?
- What kinds of information are focused on in training? Just the basics or beyond?
- Discuss the local decisions made about cataloging records in RDA and offer explanations about the decisions when necessary.
- Who will gather feedback from public services? How will that information affect implementation? For example, will the feedback and results from the searching exercise affect future changes and local decisions? If so, how?

Phase 3b: Prepare for the Future

The development of RDA has taken many years. Even during the testing stages, libraries saw this new cataloging standard change and grow. As with any major shift, change brings both possibilities and challenges. Our ultimate goal is to aid users of our libraries as they *find, identify, select,* and *obtain* information and resources.

RDA continues to evolve. The introduction of RDA and its implementation into a library's catalog is only the first step. Additional developments, including BIBFRAME and experiments with FRBR-ized catalogs, will influence future paths. How will you continue to prepare for RDA? How will you *find out* about new RDA developments, *identify* possible trouble spots in your local catalog, *select* RDA options that fit the needs of your staff and patrons, and *obtain* RDA resources? Preparing for the future with RDA means staying current with new developments, creating an environment that is able to respond and adapt, and continuing to evolve as RDA unfolds.

Exercise 4.1

Identifying DVDs in a Catalog

Examples of AACR2 and RDA records are shown for DVDs.

1. Circle the parts of each record that would be used to identify the item as a DVD.

2. Compare the AACR2 and RDA records.

3. Answer the questions:
   a. What are the differences?
   b. What are the similarities?

Example AACR2 Records

Title:	Malcolm X [videorecording]
Author:	Lee, Spike.
Publication Information:	Burbank, CA: Warner Home Video, ©2000.
Physical Description:	1 videodisc (201 min.): sd., col.; 4 ¾ in.

Title:	The hobbit [videorecording] : an unexpected journey
Author:	Nesbitt, James, 1965-
Publication Information:	Burbank, CA : Warner Home Video, ©2013.
Physical Description:	2 videodiscs (169 min.) : sd., col. ; 4 3/4 in.

Example RDA Records

Title:	Fish, mercury, and nutrition: the net effects
Author:	Groenewold, Gerald H.
Publication Information:	[Fargo, N.D.]: Prairie Public Broadcasting; [Grand Forks, N.D.]: Energy & Environmental Research Center, University of North Dakota, 2011, ©2011.
Physical Description:	1 videodisc (30 min.): color, sound; 4 3/4 in.

Title:	Lincoln
Author:	Spielberg, Steven, 1946- director, producer
Publication Information:	Universal City, Calif: Dreamworks pictures, ©2013
Physical Description:	1 videodisc (approximately 150 min.) : color, sound ; 4 3/4 in.

Worksheet 4.1: Factoring Staff Time and Cost

Library Name				
Length of Time for Implementation of RDA, estimating total number of hours				
Staff Name	**Title & Duties**	**Role/Involvement with RDA**	**Project Hours**	**Cost***

Earnings per hour × project hours

Answers to Mini-Exercises

Mini-Exercise 1.2: *w, e, m, or i?*

1. item (i)
2. expression (e)
3. manifestation (m)
4. expression (e)
5. work (w)
6. manifestation (m)
7. item (i)

Mini-Exercise 1.3: *Where in RDA will I find X?*

1. c) manifestation
2. RDA 3.5.2.2
   The path to the answer through the RDA Table of Contents:
   Section 1: Recording attributes of manifestation & item
       Chapter 3: Describing carriers
           3.5 Dimensions
               3.5.2 Dimensions of map, etc.
                   3.5.2.2 Recording dimensions of maps, etc.
3. b) expression
4. RDA 7.16.1
   The path to the answer through the RDA Table of Contents:
   Section 2: Recording attributes of work & expression
       Chapter 7: Describing content
           7.16 Supplementary content
               7.16.1 Basic instructions on recording supplementary content
5. a) work
6. RDA 6.3.1
   The path to the answer through the RDA Table of Contents:
   Section 2: Recording attributes of work & expression

Chapter 6: Identifying works and expressions
6.3 Form of work
6.3.1 Basic instructions on recording form of work

Mini-Exercise 2.1: *What Are You Cataloging?*

1. c
2. d
3. e
4. b
5. a

Mini-Exercise 2.2: *What Do You See?*

1. RDA core
2. Neither
   Explanation: Other title information is core for LC, but is not RDA Core.
3. RDA core
4. RDA core
5. Neither
   Explanation: Relationship designators are optional.
6. Neither
   Explanation: While contributors are not a core element of RDA, providing them as additional access points is helpful in completing the find, identify, and select user tasks.
7. RDA core-if
   Explanation: Copyright date is core if there is not a date of publication or distribution.
8. RDA core
9. RDA core
10. RDA core

Mini-Exercise 2.3: *What Do You Record?*

*Note: changes to the MARC fields are shown in **bold**.*

1. 300 _ _ $a 57 pages : $b illustrations (some **color**) ; $c 22 cm
2. 300 _ _ $a xii, 492 **pages** : $b **illustrations** ; $c 28 cm
3. 300 _ _ $a 1 **volume** (unpaged) : $b chiefly color illustrations ; $c 25 cm.
   490 _ _ $a Long lost book series
4. 504 _ _ $a Includes bibliographical references (**pages** 219–223) and index.

Mini-Exercise 3.1: *Persons and Families*

1. b) Sandford, John, 1944 February 23–
   Explanation: If more than one person has the same name and is born in the same year, the month and the day of birth are included as part of access points. Complete dates are listed as year-month-date. Months are not abbreviated. Most abbreviations are no longer used with access points. See RDA 9.3.2.3.
2. a) Madonna, 1958–
   Explanation: The name by which the person is most commonly known is generally chosen as the preferred name. See RDA 9.2.2.3.
3. c) O'Keefe, James (Automobile racing historian)
   Explanation: If a fuller form of the name and dates of a person are unknown or if the name does not convey the idea of a person, the person's occupation or profession can be added to the name. A person's occupation or profession is always enclosed in parenthesis. Topical subject headings are not used as qualifiers. See RDA 9.19.1.4-9.19.1.6.
4. a) Pasquali, Nicolo, approximately 1718–1757
   Explanation: When actual birth or death dates are uncertain, approximate *is used before the date. Latin abbreviations are not used in RDA. See RDA 9.3.1.3.*
5. b) Calder (Family : 1757–1959 : N.C.)
   Explanation: Type of family is an RDA core element and must be included as part of the access point. See RDA 10.3.

Mini-Exercise 3.2: *Corporate Bodies*

1. a) Nebraska. Department of Social Services
   Explanation: As with names of persons, the preferred name for a corporate body is the most commonly known form. The spelled out form of Department *is used instead of the abbreviation* Dept. *See RDA 11.2.2.*
2. b) Advances in Computer Games (Conference) (10th : 2003 : Graz, Austria)
   Explanation: The number of the conference does not appear in the authorized access point. It is part of the conference's qualifier. Numbers are recorded as ordinal numbers (i.e., 1st, 2nd). See RDA 11.6.
3. a) 10 Mile Crossing (Musical group)
   Explanation: When the name of a corporate body does not convey the idea of a corporate body, a word or a phrase qualifier can be used. See RDA 11.7.1.4.
4. b) St. Mark's Episcopal Church (Evanston, Ill.)
   Explanation: The Library of Congress's authority file includes more than 10 churches called St. Mark's Episcopal Church. When you need to distinguish a corporate body from another corporate body with the same name, the place associated with the corporate body is a core element. See RDA 11.3.

Mini-Exercise 3.3: *Works and Expressions*

1. c) Bible. Revelation

   Explanation: RDA uses the spelled out forms of Old Testament *and* New Testament *instead of* O.T. *and* N.T. *The name of the testament is omitted from the preferred titles of individual books or groups of books. See RDA 6.23.2.9.*

2. a) Barney Miller (Television program)

   Explanation: The preferred titles of motion pictures and television and radio programs include forms of the works. These terms are added in parentheses to the preferred title. They are added to help convey the idea of a motion picture, television program, and radio program. See RDA 6.3.

3. b) Lewis, C. S. (Clive Staples), 1898–1963. Works. Selections

   Explanation: For compilations, which consist of two or more works of a single author, but are not all their publications, Work. Selections *is added to the preferred title. Under AACR2, the word* Selections *was used alone for selected publications of writers who wrote in more than one format. See RDA 6.2.2.10.3.*

4. b) Lenski, Lois, 1893–1974. Cowboy Small. Spanish

   d) Lenski, Lois, 1893–1974. Cowboy Small. English

   Explanation: If the original English language expression and the Spanish translation are published as a compilation, an analytical authorized access point is given for each expression. Under AACR2, the different expressions is given together in subfield $l of uniform title MARC field 240. See RDA 6.11.

Answers to Exercises

Exercise 1.1: *Work, Expression, Manifestation, or Item?*

Note: Your outline or diagram may differ from what is shown here. For example, the expression labeled here as "e_1" may be labeled as "e_2" or "e_7" in your outline. Perhaps you consider the movie to be an expression of C.S. Lewis's The Lion, the Witch, and the Wardrobe, *instead of a separate but related work. The basic details of your outline or diagram likely match the outline here. When they differ, justify your choices.*

w_1 C. S. Lewis's *The Lion, the Witch, and the Wardrobe*

    e_1 the original English text with illustrations by Pauline Baynes

        m_1 the book published in 1950 by Geoffrey Bles

            i_1 copy 1 in Special Collections

            i_2 copy 2 in the Reserve Collection

        m_2 the book published in 1950 by Macmillan

            i_3 copy 1 in the Adult Fiction Collection

            i_4 copy 2 in Preservation; back cover damaged

        m_3 the paperback book published in 1994 by HarperCollins

            i_5 copy 1 in the Young Adult Fiction Collection

            i_6 copy 2 in the Young Adult Fiction Collection

            i_7 copy 3 in the Adult Fiction Collection

        m_4 the library binding book published in 1994 by HarperCollins

            i_8 copy in the Young Adult Fiction Collection

        m_5 the large print book published in 1987 by Scholastic

            i_9 copy in the Large Print Collection

    e_2 the Spanish translation by Teresa Mlawer

        m_6 the book published in 2002 by HarperCollins

            i_{10} copy in the Spanish Language Collection

        m_7 the eBook published in 2002 by HarperCollins

            i_{11} copy accessible through library website

    e_3 spoken word in English, unabridged, read by Michael York

        m_8 the downloadable audiobook released in 2005 by Harper Audio

            i_{12} copy accessible through library website

        m_9 the CDs released in 2006 by HarperCollins

           i_{13} copy 1 in the Audiovisual Collection

           i_{14} copy 2 in the Audiovisual Collection

        m_{10} the Playaway released in 2007 by Playaway Digital Audio

           i_{15} copy in the Audiovisual Collection

    e_4 spoken word in English, unabridged, read by a full cast from BBC radio

        m_{11} the downloadable audiobook released in 2006 by BBC Audio-books

           i_{16} copy accessible through library website

w_2 the movie *The Chronicles of Narnia: The Lion, the Witch, and the Wardrobe*

    e_5 the motion picture presented by Walt Disney Pictures and Walden Media

        m_{12} the film reels and sound discs released in 2005 by Buena Vista Pictures

           i_{17} copy in Special Collections

        m_{13} the DVD distributed by Buena Vista Home Entertainment in 2005

           i_{18} copy 1 in the Audiovisual Collection

           i_{19} copy 2 in the Audiovisual Collection

        m_{14} the Blu-ray distributed by Buena Vista Home Entertainment in 2008

           i_{20} copy in the Audiovisual Collection

w_3 the video game *The Chronicles of Narnia: The Lion, The Witch, and the Wardrobe*

    e_6 the interactive multimedia version presented by Disney and Walden Media

        m_{15} the CD-ROMs released in 2005 by Buena Vista Games

           i_{21} copy in the Reserve Collection for in-library use

w_4 Leland Ryken and Marjorie Lamp Mead's *A Reader's Guide Through the Wardrobe: Exploring C.S. Lewis's Classic Story*

    e_7 the original English text

        m_{16} the book published in 2005 by InterVarsity Press

           i_{22} copy in the Nonfiction Collection

Explanation: These resources center around the work The Lion, the Witch, and the Wardrobe *(w_1). Three additional works are related to w_1: a work in the form of a movie (w_2), a work in the form of a video game (w_3), and Ryken and Mead's* A Reader's Guide through the Wardrobe *(w_4). The movie (w_2) differs enough from C. S. Lewis's* The Lion, the Witch, and the Wardrobe *(w_1) to justify labeling it as a new work (w_2) instead of an expression of w_1.*

    Of the four expressions of C. S. Lewis's The Lion, the Witch, and the Wardrobe *(w_1), two are expressed via text (e_1, e_2) and two through spoken word (e_3, e_4). The*

original English text with illustrations by Pauline Baynes (e_1) has multiple manifestations that differ according to publisher, publication date, print size, and binding or cover type. The Spanish translation (e_2) has two manifestations divided by print (m_6) and eBook format (m_7). The two spoken word expressions (e_3, e_4) are read by different people. The Michael York performance is available in three manifestations: a downloadable audiobook (m_8), CDs (m_9), and Playaway (m_{10}).

The movie (w_2) has a single expression (e_5), but that expression is manifested in film reels (m_{12}), DVDs (m_{13}), and Blu-ray (m_{14}).

Both the video game (w_3) and Ryken and Mead's A Reader's Guide through the Wardrobe *(w_4) have a single expression, a single manifestation, and a single item available through the library.*

Finally, the library owns one to three items for each manifestation and houses them in various physical and online collections.

Exercise 1.2: *Entities, Attributes, and Relationships*

Part 1: *Entities and Attributes*

1. m (Title of the manifestation, Statement of responsibility)
2. m (Place of publication, Publisher, Date of publication)
3. m (Extent of the carrier, Dimensions of the carrier)
4. e (Content type)
5. m (Media type)
6. m (Carrier type)
7. m (Series statement)
8. e (Supplementary content)
9. e (Summarization of the content)
10. m (Manifestation identifier)
11. i (Item identifier)
12. i (Marks/inscriptions)

Part 2: *Entities and Relationships*

1. b) Group 2
2. d) item
3. c) Group 3
4. a) work
5. c) manifestation

Exercise 1.3: *Navigating the RDA Table of Contents*

1. c) manifestation

    RDA 2.8.4.5   More than one publisher

2. b) expression
   RDA 7.16.1   Basic instructions on recording supplementary content
3. c) manifestation
   RDA 2.12.2.3   Recording title proper of series
4. c) manifestation
   RDA 2.8.2.3   Recording place of publication
5. b) expression
   RDA 6.9.1   Basic instructions on recording content type
6. c) manifestation
   RDA 3.2.1   Basic instructions on recording media type
7. c) manifestation
   RDA 3.3.1   Basic instructions on recording carrier type
8. c) manifestation
   RDA 2.15.1   Basic instructions on recording identifiers for the manifestation
9. c) manifestation
   RDA 3.4.1   Basic instructions on recording extent
10. c) manifestation
    RDA 3.5.1.4.14 Volumes
11. b) expression
    RDA 7.17.1.4   Details of color content
12. c) manifestation
    RDA 2.4.1.6   More than one statement of responsibility
13. d) item
    RDA 2.19.1   Basic instructions on recording identifiers for the item
14. a) work
    RDA 7.7.1   Basic instructions on recording the intended audience
15. b) expression
    RDA 7.10.1   Basic instructions on summarizing the content
16. d) item
    RDA 4.5.1   Basic instructions on recording restrictions on use
17. c) manifestation
    RDA 2.7.1   Basic instructions on recording production statements
18. c) manifestation
    RDA 2.3.6.3   Recording variant titles
19. b) expression
    RDA 7.23.1   Basic instructions on recording performers, narrators, and/or presenters
20. a) work
    RDA 6.3.1   Basic instructions on recording form of work

Exercise 2.1: *Cataloging with RDA*

Book 1: Worksheet A—What Are You Cataloging?	
Element	**Data**
Mode of Issuance	single-unit
Content Type	text
Media Type	unmediated
Carrier Type	volume
Preferred Source of Information	title page

Book 1: Worksheet B—What Do You See?	
Element	**Data**
Title Proper	Building Castles and Other Magical Spaces
Other Title Information	the architecture of a wizarding world
Statement of Responsibility Relating to Title Proper	Nora Peterson ; photo-illustrations by Miranda K. Abbe
Creator	Peterson, Nora
Relationship Designator	author
Contributor	Abbe, Miranda K.
Relationship Designator	illustrator
Place of Publication	Melbourne
Publisher's Name	PANDA PRESS
Date of Publication	2013
Copyright Date	*Not applicable*
Designation of Edition	*Not applicable*
Title Proper of Series	*Not applicable*
Numbering within Series	*Not applicable*
Identifier for the Manifestation	9780104112001

Book 1: Worksheet C—What Do You Record?	
Element	**Data**
Extent	250 pages
Illustrative Content	color illustrations
Dimensions	30 cm
Note	Includes bibliographical references (pages 240-245) and index
Language of the Content	eng

Book 1: Worksheet D—RDA in MARC										
LDR/06 (Type)	**a**	Elvl		Srce		Audn		Ctrl		Lang **eng**
LDR/07 (BLvl)	**m**	Form		Conf	0	Biog		Mrec		Ctry at
		Cont	b	GPub		LitF	0	Indx	1	
LDR/18 (Desc)	**i**	Ills	a	Fest	0	DtSt	s	Dates	2013,	

040 _ _	$a ### $b eng $e **rda** $c ###
020 _ _	$a 9780104112001
100 1 _	$a Peterson, Nora, $e author.
245 1 0	$a Building Castles and Other Magical Spaces : $b the architecture of a wizarding world / $c Nora Peterson ; photo-illustrations by Miranda K. Abbe.
264 _ 1	$a Melbourne : $b PANDA PRESS, $c 2013.
300 _ _	$a 250 pages : $b color illustrations ; $c 30 cm
336 _ _	$a text $2 rdacontent
337 _ _	$a unmediated $2 rdamedia
338 _ _	$a volume $2 rdacarrier
504 _ _	$a Includes bibliographical references (pages 240-245) and index.
700 1 _	$a Abbe, Miranda K., $e illustrator.

Book 2: Worksheet A—What Are You Cataloging?	
Element	**Data**
Mode of Issuance	single-unit
Content Type	text
Media Type	unmediated
Carrier Type	volume
Preferred Source of Information	title page

Book 2: Worksheet B—What Do You See?	
Element	**Data**
Title Proper	first steps
Other Title Information	*Not applicable*
Statement of Responsibility Relating to Title Proper	MAX DUST
Creator	Dust, Max
Relationship Designator	author
Contributor	*Not applicable*
Relationship Designator	*Not applicable*
Place of Publication	Ashland, NE*
Publisher's Name	wild things publishing
Date of Publication	[2013]
Copyright Date	©2013
Designation of Edition	FIRST EDITION
Title Proper of Series	*Not applicable*
Numbering within Series	*Not applicable*
Identifier for the Manifestation	9780104272012

*Alternative Answer: Ashland, NE ; Des Moines, IA
[first named place of publication is required, additional places of publication are optional]

Book 2: Worksheet C—What Do You Record?	
Element	**Data**
Extent	xii, 237 pages
Illustrative Content	illustrations
Dimensions	21 cm
Note	Includes index
Language of the Content	eng

Book 2: Worksheet D—RDA in MARC

LDR/06 (Type)	a	Elvl		Srce		Audn		Ctrl		Lang	**eng**
LDR/07 (BLvl)	m	Form		Conf	0	Biog		Mrec		Ctry	nbu
		Cont		GPub		LitF	0	Indx	1		
LDR/18 (Desc)	i	Ills	a	Fest	0	DtSt	s	Dates	2013,		

040 _ _	$a ### $b eng $e **rda** $c ###
020 _ _	$a 9780104272012
100 1 _	$a Dust, Max, $e author.
245 1 0	$a first steps / $c MAX DUST.
250 _ _	$a FIRST EDITION.
264 _ 1	$a Ashland, NE : $b wild things publishing, $c [2013]
300 _ _	$a xii, 237 pages : $b illustrations ; $c 21 cm
336 _ _	$a text $2 rdacontent
337 _ _	$a unmediated $2 rdamedia
338 _ _	$a volume $2 rdacarrier
500 _ _	$a Includes index.

Book 3: Worksheet A—What Are You Cataloging?	
Element	**Data**
Mode of Issuance	single-unit
Content Type	text
Media Type	unmediated
Carrier Type	volume
Preferred Source of Information	title page

| Book 3: Worksheet B—What Do You See? ||
Element	Data
Title Proper	DOUBLE DRIBBLE
Other Title Information	MY LIFE IN BASKETBALL
Statement of Responsibility Relating to Title Proper	Erik Bowman and Ben Bornkamp
Creator	Bowman, Erik
Relationship Designator	author
Contributor	Bornkamp, Ben
Relationship Designator	author
Place of Publication	[Place of publication not identified]
Publisher's Name	Amazing ALLSTARS
Date of Publication	[2014]
Copyright Date	©2014
Designation of Edition	First ALLSTAR edition
Title Proper of Series	*Not applicable*
Numbering within Series	*Not applicable*
Identifier for the Manifestation	9780204232010 (hardcover) 9780220100423 (paperback)

| Book 3: Worksheet C—What Do You Record? ||
Element	Data
Extent	160 pages
Illustrative Content	illustrations (some color)
Dimensions	22 cm
Note	*Not applicable*
Language of the Content	eng

Book 3: Worksheet D—RDA in MARC											
LDR/06 (Type)	**a**	Elvl		Srce		Audn		Ctrl		Lang	**eng**
LDR/07 (BLvl)	**m**	Form		Conf	0	Biog		Mrec		Ctry	xx
		Cont		GPub		LitF	0	Indx	0		
LDR/18 (Desc)	**i**	Ills	a	Fest	0	DtSt	s	Dates	2014,		

040 _ _	$a ### $b eng $e **rda** $c ###
020 _ _	$a 9780204232010 (hardcover)
020 _ _	$a 9780220100423 (paperback)
100 1 _	$a Bowman, Erik, $e author.
245 1 0	$a DOUBLE DRIBBLE : $b MY LIFE IN BASKETBALL / $c Erik Bowman and Ben Bornkamp.
250 _ _	$a First ALLSTAR edition.
264 _ 1	$a [Place of publication not identified] : $b Amazing ALLSTARS, $c [2014]
300 _ _	$a 160 pages : $b illustrations (some color) ; $c 22 cm
336 _ _	$a text $2 rdacontent
337 _ _	$a unmediated $2 rdamedia
338 _ _	$a volume $2 rdacarrier
700 1 _	$a Bornkamp, Ben, $e author.

Book 4: Worksheet A—What Are You Cataloging?	
Element	Data
Mode of Issuance	single-unit
Content Type	text
Media Type	unmediated
Carrier Type	volume
Preferred Source of Information	title page

Book 4: Worksheet B—What Do You See?	
Element	**Data**
Title Proper	DAUGHTERS OF THOR
Other Title Information	*Not applicable*
Statement of Responsibility Relating to Title Proper	D. Dillon Halas
Creator	Halas, D. Dillon
Relationship Designator	author
Contributor	*Not applicable*
Relationship Designator	*Not applicable*
Place of Publication	Athens*
Publisher's Name	mythbooks
Date of Publication	2013
Copyright Date	*Not applicable*
Designation of Edition	mythbooks edition
Title Proper of Series	BRIDGE TO VALHALLA
Numbering within Series	Book three
Identifier for the Manifestation	9780203062004
*Alternative Answer: Athens, Rome, Oslo [first named place of publication is required, additional places of publication are optional]	

Book 4: Worksheet C—What Do You Record?	
Element	**Data**
Extent	233 pages
Illustrative Content	*Not applicable*
Dimensions	22 cm
Note	*Not applicable*
Language of the Content	eng

Book 4: Worksheet D—RDA in MARC										
LDR/06 (Type)	**a**	Elvl		Srce		Audn		Ctrl		Lang	**eng**
LDR/07 (BLvl)	**m**	Form		Conf	0	Biog		Mrec		Ctry	it
		Cont		GPub		LitF	0	Indx	0		
LDR/18 (Desc)	**i**	Ills		Fest	0	DtSt	s	Dates	2013,		

040 _ _	$a ### $b eng $e **rda** $c ###
020 _ _	$a 9780203062004
100 1 _	$a Halas, D. Dillon, $e author.
245 1 0	$a DAUGHTERS OF THOR / $c D. Dillon Halas.
250 _ _	$a mythbooks edition.
264 _ 1	$a Athens : $b mythbooks, $c 2013.
300 _ _	$a 233 pages ; $c 22 cm.
336 _ _	$a text $2 rdacontent
337 _ _	$a unmediated $2 rdamedia
338 _ _	$a volume $2 rdacarrier
490 0 _	$a BRIDGE TO VALHALLA ; $v Book three

Book 5: Worksheet A—What Are You Cataloging?	
Element	**Data**
Mode of Issuance	single-unit
Content Type	text
Media Type	unmediated
Carrier Type	volume
Preferred Source of Information	title page

Book 5: Worksheet B—What Do You See?	
Element	**Data**
Title Proper	Easter Egg Hunt
Other Title Information	*Not applicable*
Statement of Responsibility Relating to Title Proper	Written by Mikela Kralman ; Pictures by Beatrice Kiffmeyer
Creator	Kralman, Mikela
Relationship Designator	author
Contributor	Kiffmeyer, Beatrice
Relationship Designator	illustrator
Place of Publication	Gretna, Nebraska
Publisher's Name	[publisher not identified]
Date of Publication	2013
Copyright Date	*Not applicable*
Designation of Edition	*Not applicable*
Title Proper of Series	*Not applicable*
Numbering within Series	*Not applicable*
Identifier for the Manifestation	9780120060630

Book 5: Worksheet C—What Do You Record?	
Element	**Data**
Extent	approximately 30 pages
Illustrative Content	color illustrations
Dimensions	20 cm
Note	*Not applicable*
Language of the Content	eng

Book 5: Worksheet D—RDA in MARC								
LDR/06 (Type)	**a**	Elvl	Srce	Audn	Ctrl		Lang	**eng**
LDR/07 (BLvl)	**m**	Form	Conf 0	Biog	Mrec		Ctry	nbu
		Cont	GPub	LitF 0	Indx 0			
LDR/18 (Desc)	**i**	Ills a	Fest 0	DtSt s	Dates 2013,			

040 _ _	$a ### $b eng $e **rda** $c ###
020 _ _	$a 9780120060630
100 1 _	$a Kralman, Mikela, $e author.
245 1 0	$a Easter Egg Hunt / $c Written by Mikela Kralman ; Pictures by Beatrice Kiffmeyer.
264 _ 1	$a Gretna, Nebraska : $b [publisher not identified], $c 2013.
300 _ _	$a approximately 30 pages : $b color illustrations ; $c 20 cm
336 _ _	$a text $2 rdacontent
337 _ _	$a unmediated $2 rdamedia
338 _ _	$a volume $2 rdacarrier
700 1 _	$a Kiffmeyer, Beatrice, $e illustrator.

Exercise 3.1: Understanding Authority Records

A.
1. November 29, 1898
2. November 22, 1963
3. Belfast, Northern Ireland; Oxford, England
4. author; scholar; broadcaster
    Explanation: MARC field 374 is repeatable. For some authority records, a person's occupations are listed in multiple 374s instead of one 374, as shown in this record.
5. Oxford University; Cambridge University
    Explanation: Subfield $a of MARC field 373 is repeatable. For some authority records, a person's occupations are listed in a single 373 instead of multiple 373s, as shown in this record.
6. Lewis, Jack, 1898-1963; Hamilton, Clive, $d 1898-1963; Clerk, N. W., 1898-1963; Lewis, Clive Staples, $d 1898-1963

B.
1. August 28, 1971
2. Nice, France
3. Paris, France
4. comics artist and creator; film director

Explanation: Subfield $a of MARC field 374 is repeatable. For some authority records, a person's occupations are listed in a single 374 instead of multiple 374s, as shown in this record.

5. male

C.
1. July 29, 1880
2. July 25, 1971
3. Riverside, Calif.; San Bernardino, Calif.
4. 1909-1915
5. Brooklyn Robins; Boston Braves
   Explanation: Subfield $a of MARC field 373 is repeatable. For some authority records, a person's occupations are listed in a single 373 instead of multiple 373s, as shown in this record.
6. Meyers, John Tortes

D.
1. 2000 D Street, Lincoln, Neb. U.S. 68502
   Explanation: $v of MARC field 371 tells where the address of the church was found.
2. 1923, 1931
3. First Congregational Church (organized 1866) and Plymouth Congregational Church (organized 1887)
4. First-Plymouth Congregational Church (Lincoln, Neb.); First-Plymouth Congregational Church UCC (Lincoln, Neb.)
5. United Church of Christ
   Explanation: $2 tells the source of the term United Church of Christ (i.e., Library of Congress's Name Authority File).

E.
1. 1962
2. Jagger, Mick; Richards, Keith,
3. London, England
4. Stones (Musical group); The Rolling Stones; The Stones (Musical group); Strolling Bones (Musical group); The Strolling Bones (Musical group)
5. Rock music; Blues (Music); Blues-rock music; Rhythm and blues music
   Explanation: MARC field 372 is repeatable. For some authority records, a corporate body's fields of activity are listed in multiple 372s instead of a single 372, as shown in this record.

F.
1. South Portland, Me.
2. Cass, Malcolm Walter, 1916-2008
3. NUCMC data from Maine Hist. Soc. for Its Collection

G.

1. July 19-23, 2010
2. Dartmouth College

H.

1. a. Poems
   c. Correspondence

Exercise 4.1: Identifying DVDs in a Catalog

1. [videorecording], Videodisc, Color, sound, sd., col.
3. **a. Differences**: [videorecording] is omitted, words are spelled out in RDA, publication information includes produced and copyright dates when it is the same date, relationship designators are present
   b. Similarities: Videodisc still used, Author and Title are still the same at the base

Glossary

Ruth Carlock

Access point—"A name, term, code, etc. under which information pertaining to a specific entity will be found" (RDA Glossary).

Attribute—"Characteristic of an entity. An attribute can be inherent in an entity or externally imputed" (ICP Glossary).

Authorized access point—"The standardized access point representing an entity" (RDA Glossary).

Carrier—"A physical medium in which data, sound, images, etc., are stored. For certain types of resources, the carrier may consist of a storage medium (e.g., tape, film) sometimes encased in a plastic, metal, etc., housing (e.g., cassette, cartridge) that is an integral part of the resource" (RDA Glossary).

Carrier type—"A categorization reflecting the format of the storage medium and housing of a carrier in combination with the type of intermediation device required to view, play, run, etc., the content of a resource" (RDA Glossary).

Content type—"A categorization reflecting the fundamental form of communication in which the content is expressed and the human sense through which it is intended to be perceived. For content expressed in the form of an image or images, content type also reflects the number of spatial dimensions in which the content is intended to be perceived and the perceived presence or absence of movement" (RDA Glossary).

Contributor—"A person, family, or corporate body contributing to the realization of a work through an expression" (RDA Glossary).

Core element—An element considered essential or requisite in RDA. A core element supports fundamental, basic user tasks. The RDA core elements, a subset of the complete RDA set, provide the minimum data required for bibliographic and authority records.

Core-if element—An element considered to be core or required in RDA only if a particular situation applies.

Corporate body—"An organization or group of persons and/or organizations that is identified by a particular name and that acts, or may act, as a unit" (RDA Glossary).

Creator—"A person, family, or corporate body responsible for the creation of a work" (RDA Glossary).

Discovery system—*See* Federated system.

Element—"A word, character, or group of words and/or characters representing a distinct unit of bibliographic information" (RDA Glossary).

Entity—Something that has a unitary and self-contained character, something that has independent or separate existence; an abstraction, ideal concept, object of thought, or transcendental object (Webster's Third New International Dictionary).

Entity relationship model—A model that organizes data using three basic constructs: entities, the attributes of entities, and relationships between entities.

Expression—"The intellectual or artistic realization of a work in the form of alpha-numeric, musical, or choreographic notation, sound, image, object, movement, etc., or any combination of such forms" (FRBR 3.2.2).

Family—"Two or more persons related by birth, marriage, adoption, civil union, or similar legal status, or who otherwise present themselves as a family" (RDA Glossary).

Federated system—A single search engine that returns relevancy-ranked results after searching multiple databases.

Group 1 entities—The FRBR entities work, expression, manifestation, and item, known collectively by the acronym WEMI. "The products of intellectual or artistic endeavor that are named or described in bibliographic records" (FRBR 3.1).

Group 2 entities—The FRBR and FRAD entities person, family, and corporate body, known collectively in this workbook by the acronym PFCb. "Those entities responsible for the intellectual or artistic content, the physical production and dissemination, or the custodianship" of works, expressions, manifestations, and items (FRBR 3.1).

Group 3 entities—The FRBR entities concept, object, event, and place, known collectively in this workbook by the acronym COEvPl. "Entities that serve as the subjects of intellectual or artistic endeavour" (FRBR 3.1).

Hybrid catalog—A local catalog that has a mixture of bibliographic and authority records that were created under different cataloging rules. For instance, some records prepared with AACR2 rules and some prepared with the RDA instructions in the same local catalog.

Identifier for the manifestation—"A character string associated with a manifestation that serves to differentiate that manifestation from other manifestations" (RDA Glossary).

ISBD—The acronym for International Standard Bibliographic Description. Standards created to improve the sharing of bibliographic records between countries.

Media—"The means used to convey information or artistic content" (RDA Glossary).

Media type—"A categorization reflecting the general type of intermediation device required to view, play, run, etc., the content of a resource" (RDA Glossary).

Mode of issuance—"A categorization reflecting whether a resource is issued in one or more parts, the way it is updated, and its intended termination" (RDA Glossary).

Monograph—"A resource that is complete in one part or intended to be completed within a finite number of parts" (RDA Glossary).

Name—"A word, character, or group of words and/or characters by which a person, family, or corporate body is known" (RDA Glossary).

Person—"An individual or an identity established by an individual (either alone or in collaboration with one or more other individuals)" (RDA Glossary).

Preferred name—"The form of name chosen as the basis for the authorized access point representing a person, family, or corporate body" (RDA Glossary).

Preferred title—"The title or form of title chosen as the basis for the authorized access point representing a work" (RDA Glossary).

RDA Toolkit—An online source that contains the RDA instructions and facilitates their use when cataloging.

Relationship designator—"A designator that indicates the nature of the relationship between entities represented by authorized access points, descriptions, and/or identifiers" (RDA Glossary).

Split files—An issue that occurs when different forms of the same access point in a catalog are filed in a browse search with intervening screens.

Statement of responsibility—"A statement relating to the identification and/or function of any persons, families, or corporate bodies responsible for the creation of, or contributing to the realization of, the intellectual or artistic content of a resource" (RDA Glossary).

Title—"A work, character, or group of words and/or characters by which a work is known" (RDA Glossary).

Title proper—"The chief name of a resource (i.e., the title normally used when citing the resource)" (RDA Glossary).

Unmediated—"Media used to store content designed to be perceived directly through one or more of the human senses without the aid of an intermediating device. Includes media containing visual and/or tactile content produced using processes such as printing, engraving, lithography, etc., embossing, texturing, etc., or by means of handwriting, drawing, painting, etc. Also includes media used to convey three-dimensional forms such as sculptures, models, etc." (RDA Glossary).

Variant access point—"An alternative to the authorized access point representing an entity" (RDA Glossary).

Variant name—"A name or form of name by which an entity is known that differs from the name or form of name chosen as the preferred name for that entity" (RDA Glossary).

Variant title—"A title by which a work is known that differs from the title or form of title chosen as the preferred title for that work" (RDA Glossary).

WEMI—An acronym for the FRBR Group 1 entities work, expression, manifestation, and item.

Work—"A distinct intellectual or artistic creation" (FRBR 3.2.1).

Z39.50—"A national and international (ISO 23950) standard defining a protocol for computer-to-computer information retrieval" (Library of Congress, "Gateway to Library Catalogs").

Manifestations Cited

Anglo-American Cataloguing Rules. 2nd ed., 2002 revision. Prepared under the direction of the Joint Steering Committee for Revision of AACR, a committee of the American Library Association, the Australian Committee on Cataloguing, the British Library, the Canadian Committee on Cataloguing, Chartered Institute of Library and Information Professionals, the Library of Congress. Chicago: American Library Association, 2002.

Association for Library Collections & Technical Services. "ALCTS Continuing Education." http://www.youtube.com/user/alctsce/ (cited May 9, 2013).

Association for Library Collections & Technical Services. "Online Learning." http://www.ala.org/alcts/confevents (cited May 9, 2013).

Association for Library Collections & Technical Services. "Webinar Archive." http://www.ala.org/alcts/confevents/past/webinar (cited May 9, 2013).

Chen, Peter Pin-Shan. "The Entity-Relationship Model: Toward a Unified View of Data." *ACM Transactions on Database Systems* 1, no. 1 (March 1976): 9–36.

Gardner, Sue Ann, and Robin Bernstein. "RDA: Preparing for the Change Together." *Library Journal*, September 27, 2012. http://lj.libraryjournal.com/2012/09/managing-libraries/rda-preparing-for-the-change-together-backtalk/ (cited April 22, 2013).

Hennely, James. "RDA Toolkit Update: February 2013," February 11, 2013. http://www.rdatoolkit.org/blog/517 (cited May 9, 2013).

IFLA Cataloguing Section and IFLA Meetings of Experts on an International Cataloguing Code. *Statement of International Cataloguing Principles*, February 2009. http://www.ifla.org/publications/statement-of-international-cataloguing-principles (cited April 29, 2013).

IFLA Study Group on the Functional Requirements for Bibliographic Records. *Functional Requirements for Bibliographic Records: Final Report*, September 1997, as amended and corrected through February 2009. http://www.ifla.org/files/assets/cataloguing/frbr/frbr_2008.pdf (cited April 29, 2013).

IFLA Working Group on Functional Requirements and Numbering of Authority Records (FRANAR). *Functional Requirements for Authority Data: A Conceptual Model*. IFLA Series on Bibliographic Control 34, edited by Glenn E. Patton. Munich: Saur, 2009.

IFLA Working Group on the Functional Requirements for Subject Authority Records (FRSAR). *Functional Requirements for Subject Authority Data (FRSAD): A Conceptual Model*, June 2010. Edited by Marcia Lei Zeng, Maja Žumer, and Athena Salaba. http://www.ifla.org/files/assets/classification-and-indexing/functional-requirements-for-subject-authority-data/frsad-final-report.pdf (cited April 29, 2013).

Joint Steering Committee for Development of RDA. *Complete Examples: Bibliographic Records.* 6JSC/RDA/Complete Examples (Bibliographic)/Revised/2012; February 13, 2012. http://www.rda-jsc.org/docs/6JSC_RDA_Complete_Examples_%28Bibliographic%29 _Revised_2012.pdf (cited May 7, 2013).

Joint Steering Committee for Development of RDA. "Frequently Asked Questions." http:// www.rda-jsc.org/rdafaq.html (cited April 22, 2013).

Joint Steering Committee for Development of RDA. "Presentations on RDA." http://www .rda-jsc.org/rdapresentations.html (cited May 8, 2013).

Library of Congress. "RDA: Resource Description & Access Training Materials." http://www .loc.gov/catworkshop/RDA%20training%20materials/index.html (cited May 9, 2013).

Library of Congress. "Gateway to Library Catalogs: Z39.50." http://www.loc.gov/z3950/ gateway.html (cited May 14, 2013).

OCLC. "OCLC RDA Policy Statement." http://www.oclc.org/rda/new-policy.en.html (cited May 9, 2013).

PCC Post-Implementation Hybrid Bibliographic Records Guidelines Task Group. *Report of the PCC Post-Implementation Hybrid Bibliographic Records Guidelines Task Group,* October 15, 2012, minor revisions February 25, 2013. http://www.loc.gov/aba/pcc/rda/RDA %20Task%20groups%20and%20charges/PCC-Hybrid-Bib-Rec-Guidelines-TG-Report .docx (cited May 9, 2013).

PCC SCT RDA Records Task Group. "RDA Record Examples." http://www.loc.gov/cat workshop/RDA%20training%20materials/SCT%20RDA%20Records%20TG/index.html (cited May 9, 2013).

Program for Cooperative Cataloging. *PCC Guidelines for the 264 Field,* June 11, 2012. http:// www.loc.gov/aba/pcc/documents/264-Guidelines.doc (cited May 3, 2013).

Program for Cooperative Cataloging. "Program for Cooperative Cataloging (PCC) Provider-Neutral E-Resource MARC Record Guidelines." http://www.loc.gov/aba/pcc/scs/ documents/PCC-PN-guidelines.html (cited May 7, 2013).

Program for Cooperative Cataloging. "RDA Training." http://www.loc.gov/aba/pcc/rda/ RDA%20Training.html (cited April 22, 2013).

RDA Music Implementation Task Force, Bibliographic Control Committee, Music Library Association. *Best Practices for Music Cataloging: Using RDA and MARC21; Draft,* February 15, 2013. http://bcc.musiclibraryassoc.org/BCC-Historical/BCC2013/RDA_Best _Practices_for_Music_Cataloging.pdf (cited May 7, 2013).

RDA Toolkit. Chicago: American Library Association; Ottawa: Canadian Library Association; London: Chartered Institute of Library and Information Professionals (CILIP), 2010-. http://www.rdatoolkit.org (cited April 29, 2013).

"RDA Toolkit Essentials." http://www.rdatoolkit.org/essentials (cited May 9, 2013).

"RDA Toolkit Pricing." http://www.rdatoolkit.org/pricing (cited May 9, 2013).

Resource Description and Access. Chicago: American Library Association; Ottawa: Canadian Library Association; London: Chartered Institute of Library and Information Professionals (CILIP), 2010-. In RDA Toolkit. http://www.rdatoolkit.org (cited April 29, 2013).

Tillett, Barbara. *What is FRBR? A Conceptual Model for the Bibliographic Universe.* Washington, DC: Library of Congress Cataloging Distribution Service, 2004. http://www.loc.gov/ cds/downloads/FRBR.PDF (cited April 29, 2013).

Webster's Third New International Dictionary of the English Language, Unabridged. Springfield, MA: Merriam-Webster, 1993.

Useful Resources

General Information about RDA and FRBR

Carlyle, Allyson. "Understanding FRBR as a Conceptual Model: FRBR and the Bibliographic Universe." *Library Resources & Technical Services* 50, no. 4 (2006): 264–73.

Coyle, Karen. "RDA Vocabularies for a Twenty-first Century Data Environment." *Library Technology Reports* 46, no. 2 (February-March 2010).

Croissant, Charles R. "FRBR and RDA: What They Are and How They May Affect the Future of Libraries." *Theological Librarianship* 5, no. 2 (July 2012): 6–22.

FRBR Review Group. "FRBR Bibliography." http://www.ifla.org/node/881 (cited May 6, 2013).

Hart, Amy. *The RDA Primer: A Guide for the Occasional Cataloger.* Santa Barbara, CA: Linworth, 2010.

Joint Steering Committee for Development of RDA. "Frequently Asked Questions." http://www.rda-jsc.org/rdafaq.html (cited May 9, 2013).

Madison, Olivia M. A. "The Origins of the IFLA Study on Functional Requirements for Bibliographic Records." *Cataloging & Classification Quarterly* 39, 3–4 (2005): 15–37.

Maxwell, Robert L. *FRBR: A Guide for the Perplexed.* Chicago: American Library Association, 2008.

Oliver, Chris. *Introducing RDA: A Guide to the Basics.* Chicago: American Library Association, 2010.

Peponakis, Manolis. "Conceptualizations of the Cataloging Object: A Critique on Current Perceptions of FRBR Group 1 Entities."*Cataloging & Classification Quarterly* 50, nos. 5–7 (2012): 587–602.

Picco, Paola, and Virginia Ortiz Repiso. "The Contribution of FRBR to the Identification of Bibliographic Relationships: The New RDA-Based Ways of Representing Relationships in Catalogs." *Cataloging & Classification Quarterly* 50, nos. 5–7 (2012): 622–40.

Weiss, Paul. J., and Steve Shadle. "FRBR in the Real World." *The Serials Librarian* 52, nos. 1–2 (2007): 93–104.

Zhang, Yin, and Athena Salaba. *Implementing FRBR in Libraries: Key Issues and Future Directions.* New York: Neal-Schuman, 2009.

RDA in Bibliographic Records

Joint Steering Committee for Development of RDA. *Complete Examples: Bibliographic Records.* 6JSC/RDA/Complete Examples (Bibliographic)/Revised/2012; February 13, 2012.

http://www.rda-jsc.org/docs/6JSC_RDA_Complete_Examples_%28Bibliographic%29_Revised_2012.pdf (cited May 7, 2013).

Library of Congress. "RDA Record Examples." http://www.loc.gov/catworkshop/RDA%20training%20materials/SCT%20RDA%20Records%20TG/index.html (cited May 9, 2013).

Library of Congress. "LC RDA Core Elements." http://www.loc.gov/aba/rda/pdf/core_elements.pdf (cited May 9, 2013).

Library of Congress. "Term and Code List for RDA Carrier Types." http://www.loc.gov/standards/valuelist/rdacarrier.html (cited May 9, 2013).

Library of Congress. "Term and Code List for RDA Content Types." http://www.loc.gov/standards/valuelist/rdacontent.html (cited May 9, 2013).

Library of Congress. "Term and Code List for RDA Media Types." http://www.loc.gov/standards/valuelist/rdamedia.html (cited May 9, 2013).

OCLC. "OCLC RDA Policy Statement." http://www.oclc.org/rda/new-policy.en.html (cited May 9, 2013).

Program for Cooperative Cataloging. "PCC Guidelines for the 264 Field." June 11, 2012. http://www.loc.gov/aba/pcc/documents/264-Guidelines.doc (cited May 3, 2013).

Program for Cooperative Cataloging. "Program for Cooperative Cataloging (PCC) Provider-Neutral E-Resource MARC Record Guidelines." http://www.loc.gov/aba/pcc/scs/documents/PCC-PN-guidelines.html (cited May 9, 2013).

Program for Cooperative Cataloging. "RDA BIBCO Standard Record (BSR) Metadata Application Profile." http://www.loc.gov/aba/pcc/scs/documents/PCC-RDA-BSR.pdf (cited May 9, 2013).

RDA Music Implementation Task Force, Bibliographic Control Committee, Music Library Association. *Best Practices for Music Cataloging: Using RDA and MARC21; Draft*. February 15, 2013. http://bcc.musiclibraryassoc.org/BCC-Historical/BCC2013/RDA_Best_Practices_for_Music_Cataloging.pdf (cited May 9, 2013).

RDA in Authority Records

Jin, Qiang. *Demystifying FRAD: Functional Requirements for Authority Data*. Santa Barbara, CA: Libraries Unlimited, 2012.

Library of Congress. "Library of Congress Authorities." http://authorities.loc.gov/ (cited May 16, 2013).

Program for Cooperative Cataloging. "RDA in NACO Training." http://www.loc.gov/catworkshop/courses/rda_naco/course%20table.html (cited April 30, 2013).

RDA Toolkit

RDA Toolkit. Chicago: American Library Association; Ottawa: Canadian Library Association; London: Chartered Institute of Library and Information Professionals (CILIP), 2010-. http://www.rdatoolkit.org (cited May 9, 2013).

"RDA Toolkit Blog." http://www.rdatoolkit.org/blog (cited May 9, 2013).

"RDA Toolkit Essentials." http://www.rdatoolkit.org/essentials (cited May 9, 2013).

"RDA Toolkit Pricing." http://www.rdatoolkit.org/pricing (cited May 9, 2013).

MARC Format

Library of Congress Network Development and MARC Standards Office. "MARC Standards." http://www.loc.gov/marc/ (cited May 22, 2013).

Library of Congress Network Development and MARC Standards Office. "RDA in MARC." http://www.loc.gov/marc/RDAinMARC.html (cited May 22, 2013).

OCLC. "Technical Bulletin 258: OCLC-MARC Format Update 2010, including RDA Changes." http://www.oclc.org/support/documentation/worldcat/tb/258/default.htm (cited May 9, 2013).

OCLC. "Technical Bulletin 260: OCLC-MARC Format Update 2011." http://www.oclc.org/support/documentation/worldcat/tb/260/default.htm (cited May 9, 2013).

OCLC. "Technical Bulletin 261: OCLC-MARC Format Update 2012." http://www.oclc.org/support/documentation/worldcat/tb/261/default.htm (cited May 9, 2013).

Hybrid Catalog

PCC Post-Implementation Hybrid Bibliographic Records Guidelines Task Group. "PCC Guidelines for Enhancing & Editing non-RDA Integrating Resources Records." http://www.loc.gov/aba/pcc/rda/PCC%20RDA%20guidelines/Hybrid-Guidelines-IRs-Post-Impl.docx (cited May 9, 2013).

PCC Post-Implementation Hybrid Bibliographic Records Guidelines Task Group. "PCC Guidelines for Enhancing & Editing non-RDA Monograph Records." http://www.loc.gov/aba/pcc/rda/PCC%20RDA%20guidelines/Hybrid-Guidelines-Monographs-Post-Impl.docx (cited May 9, 2013).

PCC Post-Implementation Hybrid Bibliographic Records Guidelines Task Group. "PCC Guidelines for Enhancing & Editing non-RDA Serial Records." http://www.loc.gov/aba/pcc/rda/PCC%20RDA%20guidelines/Hybrid-Guidelines-Serials-Post-Impl.docx (cited May 9, 2013).

PCC Post-Implementation Hybrid Bibliographic Records Guidelines Task Group. *Report of the PCC Post-Implementation Hybrid Bibliographic Records Guidelines Task Group.* October 15, 2012, minor revisions February 25, 2013. http://www.loc.gov/aba/pcc/rda/RDA%20Task%20groups%20and%20charges/PCC-Hybrid-Bib-Rec-Guidelines-TG-Report.docx (cited May 9, 2013).

Training

Association for Library Collections & Technical Services. "ALCTS Continuing Education." http://www.youtube.com/user/alctsce/ (cited May 9, 2013).

Association for Library Collections & Technical Services. "Online Learning." http://www.ala.org/alcts/confevents (cited May 9, 2013).

Association for Library Collections & Technical Services. "Webinar Archive." http://www.ala.org/alcts/confevents/past/webinar (cited May 9, 2013).

Joint Steering Committee for Development of RDA. "Presentations on RDA." http://rda-jsc.org/rdapresentations.html (cited May 8, 2013).

Library of Congress. "RDA: Resource Description & Access Training Materials." http://www.loc.gov/catworkshop/RDA%20training%20materials/index.html (cited May 9, 2013).

Program for Cooperative Cataloging. "RDA Training." http://www.loc.gov/aba/pcc/rda/RDA%20Training.html (cited May 9, 2013).

"RIMMF2." http://www.marcofquality.com/wiki/rimmf/doku.php?id=rimmf (cited Sept. 13, 2013).

Cataloging Community Support

American Library Association LinkedIn Group. http://www.linkedin.com/groups/American-Library-Association-40592 (cited May 9, 2013).

AUTOCAT. https://listserv.syr.edu/scripts/wa.exe?A0=AUTOCAT (cited May 14, 2013).

CILIP: Library, Information and Knowledge Professionals LinkedIn Group. http://www .linkedin.com/groups/CILIP-Library-Information-Knowledge-Professionals-1730267 (cited May 9, 2013).

Haider, Salman. "Resource Description & Access (RDA)." http://resourcedescription andaccess.blogspot.com/ (cited May 9, 2013).

"Nebraska RDA Practice Group." http://rdapractice.pbworks.com/w/page/50284619/ FrontPage (cited May 9, 2013).

Nebraska RDA Practice Facebook Page. https://www.facebook.com/groups/nebraskarda practice/ (cited May 9, 2013).

OCLC-Cat List. http://listserv.oclc.org/scripts/wa.exe?SUBED1=oclc-cat&A=1 (cited May 14, 2013).

PCC, CONSER, SACO, BIBCO Discussion Lists. http://www.loc.gov/aba/pcc/discussion .html (cited May 14, 2013).

RDA Cafe Facebook Page. https://www.facebook.com/groups/RDACafe/ (cited May 9, 2013).

RDA-L. http://www.rda-jsc.org/rdadiscuss.html (cited May 14, 2013).

Index

About the Editor and Contributors

MARGARET MERING is the Coordinator of Cataloging and Metadata at the University of Nebraska–Lincoln. She teaches cataloging for the School Library Science/Educational Media Program at the University of Nebraska at Kearney. She has presented workshops on RDA in Nebraska and Missouri. She is an author of a Serials Cataloging Cooperative Training Program's training manual. She received her MLS from the University of Arizona.

RUTH CARLOCK has worked at Levitt Library, York College, York, Nebraska, for 24 years and is presently the Library Director. She teaches the online Cataloging and Classification class through Central Community College in the Nebraska State Library Program. Ruth has been on the Southeast Library System Board since June 2008 and is a member of the Nebraska Library Association, the College and University section, TSRT, and ITART. She received her Master's in Information Science and Learning Technologies from the University of Missouri in 2005.

CORINNE JACOX has been the Catalog/Reference Librarian at the Creighton University Klutznick Law Library/McGrath North Mullin & Kratz Legal Research Center, Omaha, Nebraska, since 2001. She received her MLS from Emporia State University. She has taught Cataloging and Advanced Cataloging for the University of Missouri School of Information Science & Learning Technologies and the University of Nebraska at Omaha School Library/Library Science Education Programs. Prior to coming to Creighton, she was the Head of Technical Services at the Barry University Euliano Law Library in Orlando, Florida.

CASEY KRALIK is the Technical Services Librarian at Bellevue University, Bellevue, Nebraska, and has worked there since 2005. She got her Master of Arts in Library and Information Science from the University of Missouri at Columbia in 2004. In addition, Casey's past experience in libraries includes Library Director at Joslyn Art Museum and Acquisitions Assistant at Creighton University's

Law Library. At Bellevue University, she has led many projects on collection development, cataloging, archives, weeding, and serials. In 2012 Casey began the Nebraska RDA Practice Group, where she enjoyed meeting with colleagues to learn more about RDA and how librarians planned its implementation at their institutions.

MELISSA MOLL is a Catalog and Metadata Librarian at the University of Nebraska–Lincoln. She holds a Master of Arts in library and information studies from the University of Wisconsin-Madison and a Doctor of Musical Arts in organ performance and pedagogy from the University of Iowa. Prior to coming to UNL in 2012, she taught at Bethany College (Lindsborg, Kansas) and worked as an organist and director of music in Connecticut and Wisconsin.

EMILY DUST NIMSAKONT is the Cataloging Librarian at the Nebraska Library Commission in Lincoln, Nebraska. She teaches Cataloging & Classification for the University of Missouri and the University of Nebraska at Omaha. She has also worked as a reference assistant at the University of Nebraska–Lincoln, a member services coordinator at the American Quilt Study Group, and the assistant curator at the National Museum of Roller Skating. She holds a master's degree in Library Science from the University of Missouri–Columbia and a master's degree in Museum Studies from the University of Nebraska–Lincoln.

DEIRDRE ROUTT has been the Collection Processing (aka Technical Services) manager at Omaha Public Library (OPL) since 2005. Previously she was a reference librarian/cataloger with OPL, an archivist/librarian with the Douglas County Historical Society, and a contract archivist at the Union Pacific Museum Collection, all in Omaha, Nebraska. Her first professional position was as a cataloger with the Ontario Library Services in Waterloo, Ontario. She has both an MLS and MA in history from the University of Toronto.